Selfie Made

♥

your ultimate guide to
social media stardom

♥ ♥ ♥

Selfie Made

MERIDITH VALIANDO ROJAS

WEDNESDAY

BOOKS

NEW YORK

SELFIE MADE. Copyright ©2018 by Selfie Made, LLC. All rights reserved. Printed in the United States of America. For information, address St. Martin's Press, 175 Fifth Avenue, New York, N.Y. 10010.

www.wednesdaybooks.com
www.stmartins.com

Designed by Susan Walsh

The Library of Congress Cataloging-in-Publication Data is available upon request.

ISBN 978-1-250-19674-3 (trade paperback)
ISBN 978-1-250-19675-0 (ebook)

Our books may be purchased in bulk for promotional, educational, or business use. Please contact your local bookseller or the Macmillan Corporate and Premium Sales Department at 1-800-221-7945, extension 5442, or by email at MacmillanSpecialMarkets@macmillan.com.

First Edition: October 2018

10 9 8 7 6 5 4 3 2 1

For my daughters, Penelope Lane and Theodora Robin: my greatest accomplishments. May my story inspire you to be whatever you dream, to think big, and to be Selfie Made. The only limit is your imagination. And for my husband, Chris, my forever partner, cofounder, and anchor. Thank you for believing in me always.

Contents

Selfie Made:

(adj:) pronunciation: /selfi-meid/
digital entrepreneur who has used the
internet to create and launch a business

Acknowledgments

When I was seven, I asked my mom and dad if I could open a store on our front lawn. They of course said "yes," like they said to every crazy idea I had. I went door-to-door selling neighborhood newsletters and was a master lemonade-stand proprietor. When I told them I wanted to be a singer, they gave me lessons, helped me seek out connections, and listened to my not-so-great self-taught piano songs for hours as I put on concerts in the house. They believed in me and encouraged me to be all the things I dreamed. I love you, Mom and Dad.

A big shout-out to Chris for not only cofounding Digi with me but also for helping me execute all the other ideas I get in the middle of the night.

My family: my grandma, who always talked to me like I was an adult when I was a kid and taught me to believe in magic, and my grandpa, who always saw my drive and helped encourage me.

To my big sis, Jenny, who helped build my character by never letting me be the teacher when we played school or the cashier when we played store, but always was there to listen and support me and even let me sleep in her room when I couldn't fall asleep. To my brother, Christian, who stole my thunder when accompanying me to MY audition for *A Christmas Carol* on Broadway and left as Tiny Tim. The little show-stealer helped me find a different path to pursue and one meant for me. I love you both!

To Blair, Sofi, Griff, Allie, Drew, Will, Amanda, Jackie, David, Lori, Jonny, Mary, Edmundo, Katrina, and, last but not least, Prince. To all my friends who have been my cheerleaders and comic relief, you know who you are, but to name a few: Lynda, Biff, Britt, Jay, and Zum (we're on a level 20 right now!). To my REMU family, especially Jen and Jules, xo.

Thank you to Anna Miller, for introducing me to David Vigilano, who immediately got the vision for this book. Thank you to Tom Flannery, who not only became my go-to agent but also my friend and collaborator. Thank you to Eileen Rothschild, for believing in me and *Selfie Made* and working so hard with Tom and me to make it real.

I want to thank my mentors and muses, who helped shape my ideas and helped me grow: Charles Goldstuck, for sitting with me and giving me my first break, even if it didn't go further than the audition room. Brett Higgins, for jumping in and backing Digi first. Andrew Siegel, for helping me elevate the company and trusting it could be even bigger. I remember you said it takes pressure to make diamonds. Thank you to KMB, for your early support in business and in life. Thanks also to Ryan, Guy, Ori, Allen, Ben, Dari, Larry, Alex, and Nick. And to my team at 42 West, especially Sarah, Anna, Shari, and Alex!

A shout-out to all the talent who helped make the last few years so epic and exciting and also made Digi a brand. To all the talent in this book, and the ones who I've had a chance to get to know and love. You're all a part of making Digi what it is today.

My Digi team yesterday, today, and tomorrow: my right hand, Pascal, our longest-serving employee and my dearest friend. You help to keep it all together, even in the most insane and chaotic moments. Thanks to Seth, for seeing the big picture and for always having our back. Thanks to Linnea, who can manage more things than is humanely possible, and to Bryan and Kristal, even though you stopped putting the DigiSaur in our logo!

I also want to thank every Digi supporter who inspired me to write this book in the first place. You know what you want, you're go-getters, and you're making it happen! This book is yours, and I hope it helps you realize you can do anything and everything!

Selfie Made

Introduction

THIS BOOK IS GOING TO BE YOUR BEST-KEPT SECRET.

Pic of me with emojis

DEAR GEN Z:

Hi, I'm Meridith Valiando Rojas, and we're going to have so much fun.

You may know me as that DigiTour boss, which makes sense because it's the company I founded with my husband, Chris. Yes, I'm married, I have two babies, and I run a company that throws hundreds of events with your favorite social media stars every year, all over the country. But other than those little, *tiny* things, I'm just like you.

What I mean is, even though I'm adulting, my inner voice has always been, and perennially always will be, fourteen years old.

Total transparency: when I was fourteen, I was a bit of a teacher's pet. I'm a nerd; I can't help it! I've always wanted to know everything about everything. Other kids thought I was weird because I asked so many questions in class, but I wasn't trying to be weird! By definition, teachers were the ones with the answers, so they were the ones I wanted the answers from!

Here's how this relates to you: Generation Z (you if you're a teen) has

Selfie in DigiTour sweatshirt

never wanted for answers to questions. You are the first generation to have the answer to almost every question available at your fingertips. This ability, paired with our ever-improving communication technology, has led to a totally new creation: the social media influencer.

This is a topic I know a lot about, because I live it every day. With DigiTour, I work with the top social media talent. I've seen stars rise quickly and fall even quicker. And I've seen complete anonymity morph into international stardom within a matter of hours. I've learned a few things about the subject, which is why I've written a book on it. I also learned more than a few of you are interested in pursuing this path.

The invention of the internet has led to a great accessibility to knowledge and information, but that doesn't within itself lead to intelligence. Intelligence comes from the application of knowledge, and your ability to engage with it. That's a fancy way of saying you can't learn street smarts from the internet. What good are the answers if you don't know how, when, and where to use them? That's what teachers are for: they guide you through the learning process. So for the next two-hundred-plus pages, think of me as your teacher and virtual mentor. I will do my best to guide you through this wild new world of opportunity.

Every day Digi introduces me to new people and new ways to connect to

Me @ Gramercy Theatre NYC before DigiTour Summer 2017. Photo courtesy of Nicholas Mrnarevic

them. That's why I love my job so much! And it's also why I wrote this book for you. *Selfie Made* contains everything *you* want to know about how to make it big in social media. And I know that's what you really want to do (otherwise why would you be reading this book?)! So pay attention! Take notes! Get out your highlighter!

• • •

A Quick Note

Before we get started I want to point out a few key rules to follow when using the internet:

1. Whatever your parent/guardian's rules are for using the internet, follow them. Their instructions come before any/all advice you're getting in this book.

2. Don't give out your personal information, or location, to anyone you do not personally know. When it comes to strangers, assume the person on the other end is not who you think they are, and act accordingly.

3. Let your parents/guardians know what's up. If something doesn't feel right, let someone know.

4. Be courteous to others, but keep in mind there are trolls out there. They want you to be frazzled. The only way to defeat a troll is to ignore them.

> If you're good at social media,
> you're good at business.
> —NATHAN TRISKA

Selfie Made, you will soon see, is not like any other book you've ever read. Packed in these pages are tons of insider tips and tricks to help you take over the social media world. No think tank put this book together, just me: a social media obsessive who started my own company where I can do what I love. DigiTour was once just an idea I couldn't get anyone to take seriously. Now it's a multimillion-dollar company! I'll tell you how I did it, and I'll tell you about how a lot of your favorite influencers did it, too.

Photo of me backstage at DigiFest 2014

I'll give you specific advice on what actually works. The tips I share are not the boring, superficial ones posted on educational blogs. This is the real deal; this is what your favs and the biggest talent in the social media game *actually* do and have done to gain their following.

If you haven't created a social media presence yet, *Selfie Made* will guide you every step of the way. Together we will fine-tune your focus, set your goals, and put together an action-based plan to grow your following.

For those of you who have already put some work in and have the followers to show it, you'll get detailed advice on what to do next in order to grow your brand, increase engagement, and ultimately, monetize! It's not a question of what you want to be when you grow up anymore; it's what do you want to be RIGHT NOW?

The famous painter Pablo Picasso said, "Everything you can imagine is real." Where do you imagine this book can take you? A million views on your video? Getting crowned on Musical.ly? Being onstage at Digi (I'm flattered!)? Maybe you want to build a brand like your favorite creator, or build a company like your favorite internet entrepreneur? Don't let it be just a daydream off in the distance. Take it seriously: it can happen!

Feel free to engage with *Selfie Made* in whatever way suits you. You can read it straight through, or you can skip around. Highlight the advice that resonates with you, dog-ear some pages, and take copious notes in the margins. It's almost like a textbook . . . except it's for a class you really want to take. No matter your goal, this book will help demystify *how* someone becomes a social media star and will show you practical steps so you too can be an #InternetBoss and #SelfieMade.

Let's do this!

Me with my husband and cofounder, Chris Rojas, at Digi HQ, Los Angeles, shooting a spread for Fortune mag (Photograph copyright © Michael Lewis)

The Lightbulb Moment

DON'T CALL
IT A DREAM;
CALL IT A PLAN!

J-14 magazine asked me to host a Facebook Live Q&A, which I loved. It was a quick and easy way for me to connect with my brand's audience and to offer them advice.

One of the best interactions I had was with a girl who bluntly told me, "I want to get started, but I have no ideas."

First off it was a great statement because it made me do a spit take, I laughed so hard. She was being earnest but she was also really funny. But once that initial reaction faded, the absolute honesty was refreshing. Haven't we all been there?

Sometimes inspiration hits, but you can't quite land on something specific. But there are ways to get to the idea! This person wanted to be a creator but was unsure of what she wanted to create. I suggested finding a partner.

"Maybe," I said, "someone else has an idea but doesn't know quite how to make it happen. Partnerships between thinkers and doers can be the most powerful collaborations of all!"

Ideas are great and clearly essential, but they don't mean anything without execution. Lots of people can sit around and come up with ideas, but you'd be surprised at how few actually try and make them happen. At least a handful of people I met early on when I started DigiTour told me they'd had a similar idea or they wished they'd had that idea. An idea is only the first spark before a fire is lit, but it's the hard work of rubbing two sticks together that really gets a fire going. Execution is the key.

Ideas have always been my strength. My weakness is that I get distracted easily. Shiny Object Syndrome. Maybe you're familiar with it? Symptoms include watching thirty seconds of a video and quickly jumping to one of the thumbnails on the right, then opening Snapchat and scrolling for a bit, then chiming in on a group text until you remember you haven't looked at Instagram. All in less than five minutes? I can relate.

My husband (hey, Chris, wyd) is exactly the opposite. Chris is laser focused—I mean Buddhist-monk-on-the-verge-of-enlightenment focused. It works out well: when we're on tour, I'm always thinking three stops ahead, while he's focused completely on the one we're currently settling into. If you combine the two of us, we are unstoppable. He's my partner in life and my partner in business.

That's exactly what I told that girl during the *J-14* livestream. You don't have to go out and marry your partner like I did, but good things can happen when people pair up. A lot of the influencers in this book work with a partner. If you find someone who complements your strengths and weaknesses, you can both help each other succeed further than you would alone.

START DOING SOMETHING. ANYTHING.

I always wanted to be a singer-songwriter, but I had no idea how to make it a reality.

My talent level was halfway decent, and I definitely had the motivation, but I didn't know anyone in "the biz." Where do you start when you have no connections?

When I was fifteen, I decided one way to get closer to my music-business ambitions was to apply for an internship at a record label in New York. That way, I could get an inside look at how it all worked, and make friends with every single person I met. And if Madonna or Justin Timberlake *happened* to come into my office and decided to take me on tour, well that would just be an added bonus!

One day at school I skipped lunch and went to see the internship coordinator, Miss Rosemary. Her job was to hook students up with internship opportunities. Normally she only worked with seniors, but I can be pretty convincing when I want something.

"Most companies don't pay their interns anything, so they only accept college students, who can receive course credits for their work," Miss Rosemary told me.

"Sure they *say* that," I told her, "but once they see how badly I want it and how hard I'll work, they'll definitely take me! Besides, they don't need to pay me, I just want to work there!"

"Do you know anyone who works in music?" she asked. "Anyone who could help us get in the door?"

I sighed. "No."

"Well . . . We can certainly try. But don't get your hopes up!"

For the next few months, I ate lunch with Miss Rosemary in her office. We sent dozens of letters to every record label in Manhattan, big and small, explaining why I would be the perfect fit for their program. I personalized each letter, telling each recipient how much I loved whichever artists were on their label. If they didn't have any artists I really *loved,* then I'd say how much I appreciated the *artistic value* of their artists. I hand-signed every one of the letters and said a little prayer for each one before putting them in the mail.

All of that work paid off. I was offered a summer internship! It was at J Records, home to Alicia Keys (who I really loved!) and founded by music mogul Clive Davis (Google him). When Miss Rosemary told me the amazing news, I screamed so loud the assistant principal ran in to make sure I hadn't died!

That summer, I was sixteen, and I was working in "the city." My mom would drop me off at the train station in the morning (I lived in Connecticut; it was like a forty-minute train ride) and she'd pick me up at night.

Daydreaming is nice, but it also never got anyone "discovered." And no matter how much you wish it, you'll never just wake up one day with your perfect storybook job. Nearly anything you want is attainable, but usually not overnight and often not exactly as you imagined. You need to make a plan, roll up your sleeves, and get to work. The momentum of experience will change your life.

> To be Selfie Made requires action, focus, and a lot of determination . . . and a lot of DOING!

I always set my sights on what is next. I'm not saying this is a great way to live. Sometimes you get caught up and forget to enjoy the moment. You become so supercharged with the tomorrow of it all that you never really get there. That's the big secret for you planners: tomorrow is but a myth. There only ever is today. Seize the moment, make today the day you take action!

The philosophy of action can help transform the way you think about your goals. Be patient, strategic, obsessed, and extremely thick-skinned.

Keep pushing forward even if the whole world tells you to stop. Believe in yourself!

Do you believe you can do anything you can imagine? There is a certain power and confidence that accompanies that belief. You can do it; you don't need someone to do it for you. And if it's not up to someone else, you don't need to wait around. If it's only up to you to get it done, right now is a great time to start!

EVERY DAY I'M HUSTLIN'

I was noticeably the youngest employee at J Records, but I saw it as an advantage. What do old people know about lit music?

Besides, I had found something I could *do* to get me closer to what I wanted: a record deal. How I could maximize my proximity to my dream and turn it into something real. Not only was my foot in the door, my *whole body* was in the door, through security, upstairs, and in the marketing department—with my very own office. But now what?

First things first, I knew a move could not be made immediately. It had to be a well-thought-out dance. I had to dedicate the entire summer to being the best intern in the whole program, which required coming in early, leaving late, helping at events outside of work hours, and crossing off every to-do on my boss's list for me each day, with absolute precision and attention to detail.

After I cemented a good first impression, I could then give myself a little leeway to do something bold.

Life and, by extension, the pursuit of your dreams, is all about calculated risk. There are no take backs, you must assess your strategies for all possible outcomes. So at the end of that summer, as my internship was winding down and I had clocked enough hours to complete two college courses, I made my move.

I decided that the president of J Records, Charles Goldstuck, needed to know how passionate and committed I was about my future music career. I knew he was the person who I needed to believe in me and so . . . I wrote him a letter (this writing of letters is becoming a recurring theme in this book apparently). I typed each word nervously, even quoting my notes from his "Welcome Interns" speech earlier that summer. I told him in no uncertain terms that I was an artist and he needed to hear my music.

Now, it would have been fine to just pop that letter in the mail and see if he ever read it, along with the bags and bags of unsolicited submissions that—I knew firsthand—never made it out of the mailroom.

But I also knew that even if it did get to his office, his assistant sorted his mail, and she'd never give my letter priority. She'd probably read it herself and laugh at my grandiosity while she shredded it!

The only real option I had to ensure Charles got my letter was to send it to him in an interoffice mailing envelope. This was the internal mail service that many corporate offices used to send important notices, contracts, or sensitive materials from floor to floor. I didn't entirely understand why someone couldn't just get up from their desk and walk it over to the office down the hall or a few floors down but that's the way it was done. And I wasn't there to update their messaging system. I was there to get a record contract! Anything that came in an interoffice envelope was meant to be opened right away. If I sent my letter in one, Charles would likely assume it was coming from my boss!

I took a deep breath and thought about the stakes in my calculated risk. Either security would escort me out of the building for violating some ancient code of conduct, or I'd get a record deal and become a superstar. In weighing out those two options, I decided it was a risk worth taking. I put my letter in an interoffice envelope and sent it down to the executive floor.

Fifteen minutes later my phone rang. Beads of sweat collected at the nape of my neck and soaked my summer seersucker blazer (thankfully that material is forgiving).

I answered as confidently as I could. "Yes, hi, hello, this is um . . . Meridith . . ."

"Yes, hi, hello, Meridith, this is Charles' assistant, he would like to see you. Can you come down to his office?"

"I'll be right there."

I ran out of my office, yelled to my boss that I was going to talk to the president of the company, and jetted to the stairs, running like a maniac, as quickly as I could, down five flights.

I arrived at his assistant's desk, out of breath and soaked with sweat. She smiled with her mouth, but her eyes were wide with disdain.

"Why don't you take a moment, go to the bathroom and settle down?"

"Good idea. Thanks." I started running toward the women's bathroom.

"Why don't you just walk there?" she yelled out to me.

"Good idea, again. Then maybe I'll stop sweating!" I was trying to make a joke, but she seemed more grossed out than amused.

I tried to dry the sweat stains on my shirt and blazer with the hand dryer with minimal success. I smoothed my hair and took a few seconds to pump myself up in the mirror. *What is life? Is this happening?*

When I got back, Charles' assistant led me into his gargantuan suite of an office. I braced myself for a multitude of conversations.

"Have a seat," he said, and I did. "I got your letter . . ."

I didn't say anything, just smiled and nodded, trying not to be any more annoying than I assumed he thought I was.

"It was very intriguing. And now here you are, and you're so professional looking."

"I'm not sweating, I spilled water on my jacket." He ignored me, thank God.

"You need someone to believe in you if you want them to represent you. Send me your demo CD and I'll listen to it."

A demo is like a musical résumé, and I didn't have one. I hadn't done any recordings yet. "You know, it would be better if I could do it live," I suggested.

"Alright then, let's set it up."

The meeting was over, we both stood up and shook hands. I left walking on clouds.

"I guess it went well?" his assistant said.

I thanked her for her help, and took the elevator back to my office floor. I was officially scheduled to audition for J Records. I'd be playing the same piano that Alicia Keys had played! This was all real, and this was all happening.

Spoiler alert: my audition didn't go well. I played guitar and sang two original songs. I was happy with what I did, but by the time I was done, I could just feel it. I wasn't ready to be a major-label artist.

It was disappointing, but Charles was very nice about it.

"Work on your music," he said, smiling. "You know how to pitch yourself, but you're just not ready."

I didn't let it get me down. It was still an amazing experience. And it also made me think about something I'd never realized before: I didn't want to be on the stage; I wanted to be the one making the decisions. I wanted Charles's job!

Every time you put yourself out there, you get closer to either getting what you think you want, or, in my case, realizing that what you want is something different.

The nice thing about being in Gen Z is that you can now be the artist *and* be the boss. It wasn't always like that. Ten years ago, you needed a record label to get your song on the radio, and to distribute your music on a number of different platforms. There wasn't really a way to directly access your audience. Now, you can reach an audience directly. You don't need a record executive, you just need a Wi-Fi connection! You can post your own music and engage directly with your fans. That direct bond and direct distribution has revolutionized many aspects of pop culture. And it also has created a massive, growing economy around brand-new stars.

The reason I scored an audition was because I went for it. I was hungry and I wanted it so badly that I was willing to take a risk. It didn't work out the way I wanted it to, but it led me down a path that eventually led me to my perfect job: DigiTour! Are you willing to go the extra mile to grow your channel/page/ brand? Are you willing to lose something to gain something bigger? If not, there are thousands of other people who are. But none of them are just like you!

Me with Clive Davis in CosmoGirl magazine post-internship while in my first year at NYU CosmoGirl magazine

> If you're the creator,
> you're the boss.

LIGHTBULB MOMENT:
MERIDITH EDITION

DigiTour was started in 2010, but the idea began to take shape at the end of 2009.

I was going to New York University full time, while also working full time at Columbia Records in A&R (aka Artist & Repertoire aka finding and overseeing new talent).

Cramming both in was exhilarating for me. It felt like a game. Specifically, planning my schedule felt like cramming in pieces on Tetris: morning and evening classes, forty hours in the office, and then out at different clubs, checking out the new bands on any free nights I had.

My job felt like it was pretend. How could something I loved doing actually be a job?

Life at NYU was a little harder. I was among people my age, but I was also somewhat separated. To me, I had more in common with my coworkers at Columbia, even the ones old enough to be my parents.

I'd see peers in Washington Square Park in New York City, hanging in groups around a bench. Maybe one guy would have a guitar in hand, and a girl would be sitting cross-legged, arms draped across the shoulders of her boyfriend. They all wore cable-knit sweaters and they all oozed collegiate coolness. Well, not me. I was off to class, then over to the Lower East Side to check out two bands, one at Mercury Lounge and one at Pianos.

It was my job to find new artists for the label to sign, and I was good at it. In fact, I was so good, Capitol Records hired me and gave me the chance to manage an artist. To protect the innocent, I'll call him John.

Me during my scout days at Columbia Records with Jeanine Bernardini

John had *everything* going for him, except the most important part: an audience. In pre-internet days, the music business was the only platform a new artist had to stand on. You'd get signed; they would develop you, put you on the road, put you on the radio, wave their magic wands, and do whatever they could do to turn Britney Spears into BRITNEY SPEARS.

But the new and emerging platforms disrupted that concept. YouTube allowed artists to distribute themselves, grow an audience, and go directly to the fans. Sites like SoundCloud let artists post their own music and share it with everyone with a smartphone, with only the click of a button. Little did the record labels know, but this was going to change the world . . . or at least, their world.

Columbia spent a small fortune trying to help John connect to future fans (something that would never happen today) and it wasn't working; John was on the verge of getting dropped, aka getting fired, aka being told to get lost. The president of the label went over a laundry list of things we needed to do to save my client at that point: we needed a tour, we needed to increase his social following . . . and that's where I stopped listening. A big lightbulb went on over my head: *what if we put together a social media tour?* The idea of rounding up the most popular YouTube stars and slotting John in beside them got me excited. He could get on tour and onstage with them, and maybe some of the fairy dust of the social stars would rub off on him!

Not to mention this type of tour could be huge, bringing YouTubers who had millions of online followers off their computers and straight to their followers IRL.

I called John to give him the good news: I'd figured it out! After blurting out the idea, I took a deep breath to wait anxiously for his response. I was expecting "you're brilliant!" but unfortunately he didn't share my enthusiasm.

"What are you going to do, have me onstage with a cat on a keyboard?"

"These are real performers, with millions of fans! This is a killer opportunity!"

"That sounds silly," he said, and pretended he had to take another call. A week later he fired me, and soon after Capitol dropped him.

John thought there was a stigma to touring with YouTubers. It was humiliating being fired, but deep down I knew he was wrong. This idea had a lot of potential. In fact, I thought I might have had a *really* good idea. Eureka!

I went home and told Chris what I was thinking.

"What are you telling me," he said, "that you want to produce a music tour?"

Me outside our DigiTour Winter 2016 Philly stop

"Yes."

"With a bunch of people who have never been on a stage before."

"Yes!"

"Do you know how to produce a tour?" Chris asked.

"No. Do you?"

"No. But we can figure it out."

And that, my friends, is how DigiTour was born.

FIO (DID YOU FIGURE IT OUT?)

Just because you don't know how to do something doesn't mean you can't figure it out and learn by doing. Chris and I had a good amount of shared experience in the music business, but live events was not one of our skills (yet).

You don't know how to do something?

Figure it out. Make mistakes. Doing it wrong is better than not doing it at all because if you do it wrong, you'll never do it the wrong way again. If you don't do anything at all, you don't have anything to learn from.

Chris and I started by making a list of everything we would need in order to have a successful tour:

TALENT

I'd be lying if I said the first tour was "highly curated." We just rounded up the top independent channels on YouTube. It was a mixed bag, but that's how YouTube was back then. It wasn't subdivided into tons of genres with gurus and lifecasters; it was just a platform filled with diverse expression, and everyone was welcome.

This was the first wave of creators and they were as different as any co-headliners could be. We had DeStorm Power (YouTube rapper), Dave Days (YouTube's most subscribed musician at the time and hardcore Miley Cyrus enthusiast), Tay Zonday ("Chocolate Rain" singer), and Auto-Tune the News (right off their hit "Bed Intruder Song" with Antoine Dodson).

When I reach out today, everyone knows me, and they understand DigiTour. Touring has become as much a part of being a social media star as posting videos on YouTube. When we reached out only a few years ago, it was such a novel idea. Will it work? How? When? Where do we sleep? Do we make money?

It was so new, so exciting, and really so nerve-racking. But generally everyone I called to ask to go on tour with us hung up inspired and knowing this was going to change the game. Today, the first question is, "Where do I sign up?"

CREW AND A TOUR BUS

We asked around and through word of mouth found a bus company and pieced together a crew while simultaneously learning what each crewmember did and why we needed them.

When we picked up the tour bus, that's when I realized that this was all really happening. My dream of being a rock star signed to a label was coming true, in pieces: this was my tour and this was my bus. So what if my picture wasn't on the side of it, who cares? I was doing what I loved. It was a major pinch-me moment.

That wore off after a day. Technically, it wore off after a night—the first night I slept in a bottom-level bunk on a bus full of artists. The bunks were so tiny, I felt like I was sleeping in a suitcase. Superclaustro.

And then, the biggest realization, which didn't occur to me until it was too late: there is no such thing as privacy on a tour bus. In some ways, it was nice. I got to really know the guys and girls on the tour (which came in handy when writing this book).

DigiTour 2015 tour bus

In other ways, it was tough. And I'm not just talking about the food left out, dirty socks, and occasional wet beds (yes, that happened). I was in the awkward position of being the owner of the tour, which meant I had to be Mom. And I couldn't let my guard down; if someone on the tour was bugging me, I couldn't say anything to anyone; I just had to smile and keep it moving. All these people trusted in me that I could make this work. I didn't want to let them down.

DATES/ROUTING

Routing is a difficult task. It means booking the dates for the show, and creating a plan of how to get from one venue to the next. You don't want to perform in Los Angeles one night, Toronto the next, and then down to Phoenix, Arizona. A good route will make sure that doesn't happen.

I convinced an agent who was at International Creative Management (aka ICM) to take us on and help route the tour, which was a big break for us. He had other priorities, like Beyoncé, and later, Kendrick Lamar, but I twisted his arm and he took us on. Being exceptionally friendly in all situations can pay off in these kinds of ways.

MARKETING

Our very first tweet went out to zero followers: "hello world."

We did hire a publicist, and did a few interviews about our concept and why we thought it would work. But the majority of the publicity was, pretty obviously I guess, on social media. All the talent began to promote the tour via YouTube videos and Twitter, and the beginning of our social media touring business was born.

DigiTour's main goal back then was to stick our flag in the sand and shout from the moon, "DIGITOUR. WAS. HERE." No one else had done this kind of thing before, and we were proud to be first.

SIGNAGE AND MERCHANDISE ("MERCH" FOR SHORT)

In the early days, we had a dinosaur robot we lovingly called DigiSaur. DigiSaur represented something old (dinosaur) and something new (robot), since touring was one of the oldest forms of entertainment, and internet talent was a brand-new concept.

DigiSaur was our mascot, the main man on our website, and we printed his mug on T-shirts, wristbands, buttons, and posters. We pretty much printed his mug on everything except actual mugs, since Starbucks comes in its own cup.

If you sell merch, you need someone to literally sit there and sell the merch, and sometimes, if we were understaffed, that ended up being me, hawking merch while running the show. Sometimes you have to wear a lot of hats…and sell a lot of hats, too!

I'll talk more about the best ways of selling merch later on, but for a lot of talent, merch is one of the most lucrative parts of their business.

People still ask us about DigiSaur. I think he will eventually make a comeback. He was a nice dinosaur, not too bitey.

My first ever laminate, 2011

SPONSORS

Ideas only gain value when you can back them up with real stats, facts, and execution. You need to *do* to be taken seriously. That is at the heart of being Selfie Made. You can be a fantastic salesperson with extreme enthusiasm, but ideas are just thought bubbles that will drift away unless you root them in something real.

Chris and I met with rounds and rounds of investors about possibly putting money into DigiTour. One investor was the legendary manager known for handling business for Madonna, U2, and Amy Schumer. We met in his living room, which was covered in photos of him with every famous person I had ever heard of. And here I was, asking him for money. My heart started beating faster.

I spent a few minutes explaining the things we wanted to do. I talked quickly, too quickly, trying to get it all out of my mouth before he could say no.

When I finally stopped talking, he didn't say anything for a minute, and I could tell he was really trying to work it out in his head.

"Here's the problem," he said. "Right now your company is . . . cute."

Chris looked confused. "Thanks?"

"Yeah," I said, "that's nice, but I never thought of that adjective in the context of DigiTour."

"Well, I wasn't really trying to be nice. Your excitement level is endearing, and I can see you're starting to put work in, but this isn't an undeniable thing."

He didn't invest at the time, but it was okay; we cast a wide net for possible investors. Eventually, we connected with YouTube. They loved what we were doing and wrote a check to sponsor our first-ever tour.

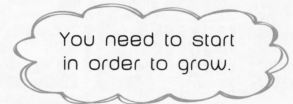

You need to start
in order to grow.

We broke so many rules when we started DigiTour. But that's why it worked. When you disrupt an existing business, you create change. This is powerful and, I must add, pretty fun.

At our very first show, the stress was real. There was just so much unknown. Was this even going to work? The audience didn't know what to expect, the talent was just as in the dark, and Chris and I were completely clueless. The whole thing was like a big experiment, like mixing two beakers of unknown origins and hoping it doesn't all blow up in your face.

Today, DigiTour events are absolute teen-dream concerts with screaming and crying and so much energy. That first show . . . was not so much. Don't get me wrong, it wasn't bad. It just wasn't a slam dunk. The energy was a little off.

We had a lot of kinks to work out, the biggest one being that since our talent was so varied in what they did, our audience was made up of vastly different types and ages of people. Grown men who came to see Auto-Tune the News didn't want to hear teens screaming when certain heartthrobs took the stage.

There were also a lot of music-industry people in the crowd. Oh, and Britney Spears (pinch me!). They came to check us out and see if we pulled it off. What they were probably seeing was their entire business model changing, and (puts science lab goggles on) life-changing realizations are known for adversely affecting an audience member's ability to engage and have a good time.

We had an idea, we went for it, and we did it. Yes, we made mistakes along the way, but we launched something and proved we had the grit and brains to actually pull it off. And even better, we had just gotten started, and you can bet your bitcoins we didn't make the same mistakes twice.

When I told you that you had to take the first step, I didn't say that step would guarantee success, or even lead in the right direction. But that step will lead you somewhere, which will lead you somewhere else, and so on, and eventually you will find what you are looking for (even if you don't know what that is). There was a little bit of awkwardness, unlike shows today, which are just high-energy love fests. That's okay! Our main goal that first night was to put on a shows and we achieved that goal. The next day, we had a new goal: put on a better show than the last one.

You are the author of your own story and no one else is going to come along and write it for you. People can help you improve your skills, give you advice, and introduce you to good connections, but ultimately it's all up to you. Maybe that feels overwhelming and intimidating, but don't let it! Let it free you! Trevor Moran, who has become one of the most famous influencers in the game, but started out as the Apple Store Dancing Kid, told me (and said to tell you), "The only person who's going to take you further is you . . . the only way you can actually make these things happen is working harder than everyone else."

If you're interested in starting out and becoming the next Miranda Sings, or founder of Musical.ly or maybe even DigiTour, then you need to take your idea and back it up with something. Go out and prove your concept. As a creator it's as simple as opening your channel, turning on your camera, filming, and posting your first vid. That first video will undoubtedly be worlds apart from your one hundredth and one thousandth videos. But it all starts with the first video, photo, or tweet. Time is sort of linear like that.

One last thing: it helps if you keep an open mind as to your end result. I was so sure I wanted to be a famous singer-songwriter. Nothing else made sense to me. But as I moved toward that goal, I inevitably learned new information, which gave me a different outlook on the world, which changed my goals.

Goals shape, shift, and transform. You're not the same person you were last year, are you? So why are you still so sure your life goals are the same this year as they were last? Don't let your goals weigh you down; let them lift you up!

THE DIGITOUR TIPPING POINT

It was 2013, and Chris and I were on tour with DigiTour 2013.

The event was hosted by O2L, Andrea Russett, and jennxpenn, and our headliners were Zoe Sugg (aka Zoella), Alfie Deyes (PointlessBlog), Tanya Burr, Jim Chapman, and Caspar Lee. It was a short tour; we were doing four nights in four cities: New York, Philadelphia, Chicago, and Toronto. This was an epic lineup, and each of our three-thousand-seat performance spaces was sold out.

The Brits were not really feeling the whole "travel by bus" thing, even though those four cities are all quite drivable destinations. No problem, we just opted for early morning flights. It went something like this: we would play a show in the early evening each night, load out by 10 or 11 P.M., get to the hotel by 12 A.M., and wake up by 3:30 A.M. to get to the airport.

To say I was tired by the last city would have been a gross understatement. Thank goodness for my floppy hat and oversize sunglasses—

Me and Zoella at the DigiTour 2013 after-party at Pod 39

the area under my eyes looked like new designer-collection bags for Chanel.

The last stop of the tour was New York City. Our show went off flawlessly, but by that point all I could think about was getting to the hotel for my first real night of sleep. The hotel had upgraded us to a beautiful room with views of the Hudson River, complimentary chocolate, and the deepest soaking bathtub I'd ever seen. As soon as the show ended and all our equipment was loaded up, Chris and I jumped in an Uber (I slept the whole ride), and I zombie walked through the hotel lobby, lay down fully clothed, and made the same mistake I always make: I checked my phone before falling asleep.

There, in my notifications, was an email from a company called Chick Launcher, a well-known women-in-business start-up pitch competition. It's now called the Women Founders Network. I had applied to their Fast Pitch competition but had never heard back. Several finalists had been given the opportunity to get in front of a room full of investors to pitch their companies.

There was one problem: the competition was the next day, and it was in Los Angeles.

My plans of sleeping in, ordering room service, and taking a long, indulgent bath were but a mere memory. I was thrilled at the opportunity to pitch DigiTour to investors, but the barely any sleep streak had to continue for one more night.

Me and Lohanthony at the DigiTour 2013 after-party at Pod 39

Chris and I packed up and changed our flights. We slept for three hours and woke up as the sun was rising, and I spent the whole five-hour plane ride building a PowerPoint presentation and prepping my pitch.

"Why don't you let me help you, babe?" Chris said through a yawn.

"It's a women-in-business competition, *babe*. How exactly would you like to help?"

With that, Chris nestled against the window and slept like a baby.

After landing twenty minutes late, we got in an Uber and raced to the hotel where the event was taking place. My hair had seen better days (like pretty much any other day) and I was wearing polka-dotted pants that *seemed* like a good idea when I bought them but now less so. And my computer, with my meticulously thought-out presentation, was on 5 percent battery.

We arrived late and out of breath. I did my best to regain my composure, but only had a few minutes before I had to begin. I plugged my laptop in . . . and the five hours of work I'd done on the plane didn't load.

How mortifying. A panel of women, all perfectly dressed, not a hair out of place, and all staring me down, waiting to see what I would do.

"I guess my presentation is gone," I said, and laughed quickly, then stopped. I wanted to keep it light, but not woman-on-the-verge-of-a-nervous-breakdown light.

None of them replied; they just kept staring. I closed my laptop and smiled. "That's okay, I don't need it anyway." I could pitch DigiTour in my sleep, which at this point I was basically doing.

I talked them through the DigiTour pitch, sans slides, and did my best to muster confidence and authority on my area of expertise. The room, initially pained by my faulty start (no one likes to witness awkwardness, so cringey), leaned in to listen to my passionate plea.

Walking out of the room, I was sure I had failed the competition, but I was really proud of my ability to pull through and get the job done. I had kept it together. If I could make it through this day, I could make it through any other day.

I walked through the lobby, looking for wherever Chris was hiding out. Before I found him, a man in an impeccable suit walked up to me.

"You're DigiTour?"

I nodded.

"I saw your presentation and I want to talk to you."

Oh. I didn't know who this was; I didn't recognize him from the pitch room. He was a big guy, over six feet and broad, and intimidating. And then I saw his name tag: Andrew Siegel. This guy was big time. He was an investor from Advance Publications (parent company of Condé Nast). I came to this competition looking for a shark, and now here I was, face-to-face with one.

"Sorry my presentation didn't load," I said.

"It didn't matter. What you're doing is interesting. I'm looking at ways to make a traditional media company relevant to younger audiences." He spoke quietly. I felt like DigiTour's future was playing out in his mind. It hadn't dawned on me that our live shows would have any relevance to a company like Condé Nast, but he saw something in Digi that I hadn't seen before. We weren't just changing the game with live performances; we were reshaping what "media" and entertainment were for younger audiences. There are not many thirteen- and fourteen-year-olds reading magazines anymore.

The investor gave me his business card and told me to call him. That's when everything changed. Condé Nast ended up coming in as our first-ever seed investor (aka our first shark). With their stamp of approval, we were able to attract investors like Ryan Seacrest and Ben Silverman (former cochairman of NBCUniversal).

Saying yes is so important to success. If I had declined the opportunity to present, if I had instead decided to get my beauty sleep, or if I had walked away when my PowerPoint wouldn't load, I wouldn't be in the position to write this book right now. Being a yes person, even when it seems like everything will go wrong, can lead to something going right! You need to be uncomfortable in order to grow.

Selfie Made Mode:

▷ Skip the middleman. Don't wait for someone to do it for you!

▷ Ideas are a new form of currency. Ideas not acted on are worth approximately $0.

▷ The first step is the first of many, so get moving!

▷ Mistakes are life's Sour Patch Kids: bitter, then sweet!

There Are Only Three Ways to Become a Social Star

Every successful social media influencer has experienced a tipping point.

There's a range of tipping points, and a variety of methods to get there. Usually a tipping point accompanies some level of virality and a dramatic change in the normal activity on an account, leading to growth at a very fast pace.

A tipping point provides the initial boost of momentum that can elevate a channel or page from user to influencer. These boosts come in a variety of forms: from no-warning-at-all viral explosion, to a feature or collaboration that provides a slight microboost. That microboost can be harnessed and expanded if you double down and work harder.

When you really break it down, there are only three methods I have ever seen work to bolster and grow social media fame:

▷ Go Viral. (Try to go viral and/or get featured)

▷ Be a Big Fish in a Small Pond. (Be early to the next big platform)

▷ Collab.

• • •

Go Viral

Okay then, I'll just go viral. Right, that is almost as silly as saying, "Go create Facebook." Gee, thanks for the advice; that was really worth the twenty-dollar book retail price, huh? We would all start something like Facebook if we could. The reality is, your odds of going *viral* are about the same as your odds of finding a unicorn with a winning lottery ticket taped to her horn (unicorn analogy activated).

This isn't a section on *how* to go viral, because if you truly go viral, that means you didn't try at all. All you did was upload something and the internet took over. Most of the biggest viral stars never cared about being famous, or even social media, for that matter.

Sudden viral fame can only be explained through the lens of someone who has gone through it, so let's look at a couple of examples:

DAMN DANIEL: A CATCHPHRASE CATCHES FIRE

In 2016 Daniel Lara and his friend Joshua Holz went viral on Twitter with a video montage of Josh complimenting Daniel on his outfit; specifically, his white Vans. The catchphrases —"Back at it again with the white Vans!" and "Dammmmn Daniel"—caught fire.

Within the first forty-eight hours the video was liked sixteen thousand times on Twitter according to Mashable. Just a few days later it had over 320,000 retweets (RT) and 460,000 likes. A day after posting the video, a few fake WorldStarHipHop accounts RT'ed the video. A pair of white Vans were posted on eBay and the bidding went up to four hundred thousand dollars. They weren't even the real shoes from the video!

Later that year, Daniel and Josh were invited to be guests on *The Ellen DeGeneres Show*, and *Time* magazine listed Daniel Lara as one of the "30 Most Influential People on the Internet."

REBECCA BLACK: FRIDAY, WHEN IT'S SO BAD IT'S VIRAL

In 2010, when Rebecca was just thirteen years old, she partnered up with an L.A. indie label called Ark Music Factory. They wrote the now viral-famous song "Friday." The song was uploaded on February 10, 2011, and received approximately one thousand views in the first month. On March 11, the video went viral, and in just a matter of days received millions of views on YouTube. It then became the most talked-about topic on Twitter. When the single was released just three days later, it sold close to forty thousand copies in the first week.

Why did "Friday" go viral? Because of how it was sold! People love clickbait and when they see the link to a video being cited as "the most terrible song in the world," curiosity gets piqued. *Billboard* called the song "auto-tuned hell," *Rolling Stone* called it an "unintentional parody of modern pop," and Perez Hilton said it was "HIGHlariously bad."

I'm sure it was hard on Rebecca to take all the hate, but she got the last laugh. She's since grown her following to over three million, released original music (much of which she wrote, and it wasn't bad!) and even a viral follow-up to "Friday," cleverly titled "Saturday."

RUNNING MAN CHALLENGE: WHEN DANCIN' GOES VIRAL

This dance fad started on Instagram as a challenge. It's basically a version of the classic nineties dance move, but with your arms closer to your body, and the song "My Boo" on the back track. Jared Nickens and Jaylen Brantley, students from the University of Maryland, made the trend mainstream. They posted on March 31, 2016. Less than a month later, there were over three thousand posts of people doing the dance.

This inspired many other basketball teams to try the dance, including Villanova, Marquette, Virginia Tech, Wisconsin, and the NCAA women's champion UConn. Soon celebs like Chris Brown were jumping on the trend and posting multiple versions of the challenge on private planes and beyond.

What Jared and Jaylen did differently was not sit around and wait for their first challenge vid to catch a headwind. Instead, they continued to post version after version of the funny-looking dance in various scenarios.

The most fascinating result of this trend was how the song playing behind each dance actually became popular again. "My Boo" reentered the Billboard Hot 100 at number twenty-nine. When it came out twenty years prior, the highest it had charted was number thirty-one!

Top Viral Dance Crazes

▶ **Gangnam Style:** In 2012, the music video for this dance hit became the first YouTube video to reach one and then two billion views.

▶ **Harlem Shake:** It was in 2013 that a series of videos were released with a masked individual and then cut to a wild party of people dancing. If you think about it, the world has never really been the same since 2013, has it?

▶ **Watch Me (Whip/Nae Nae):** I can't hear this song, released in 2015, without attempting to whip, nae nae, and do the stanky leg.

▶ **Dab:** A dance made famous by the group Migos in 2016 has now been done by most actors, sports figures . . . just about everyone has done the Dab.

▶ **Juju on That Beat (#TZAnthemChallenge):** Zay Hilfigerrr and Zayion McCall improvised the lyrics and moves to this viral classic in 2016. After posting, they were contacted by a Detroit-based group of dancing clowns (true!) known as @freshtheclowns. Hilfigerrr credits the dance troupe with turning the song into a dance challenge.

▶ Mannequin Challenge: In October of 2016, a group of students in Jacksonville, FL started the challenge by standing still while a video panned over their classroom. The following month, others joined in and synched their vids to Rae Sremmurd's "Black Beatles." The mainstream peak of this challenge was when presidential candidate Hillary Clinton accepted Jon Bon Jovi's challenge on her private plane. Also an original Beatle joined in; Paul McCartney tweeted his version of the challenge as well.

▶ TBD: The next great viral dance challenge hasn't happened yet; the internet is waiting for you to choreograph it! When you post yours, tag me!

• • •

Understanding how these favs catapulted into viral status can help provide insight as to what the process looks like, but anyone who tells you that it can be wholly re-created is lying. I will say, however, that the GO VIRAL category of social star has the challenge of combating the constant stigma of being a meme. Rebecca Black will be the first to tell you, it is not all sunshine and lollipops when the whole world is joking at your expense. When you're a meme you are not always taken seriously, in fact you're usually the butt of the joke. As quickly as you were adored and shared, people are asking if you're over yet.

Many have overcome this hurdle, like Danielle Bregoli (aka Bhad Bhabie), who now has a major record deal as a rapper and has transformed her voice into a full-blown brand, and received a Billboard Music Award nomination. But just because fame hits quickly doesn't mean it's easy to stick around. And once the perks of fame are gone, all you'll have left is the tons and tons of proof of what once was.

If you think of social media stardom like the Super Bowl, then the tipping point is the kickoff. Until then, everything that those players did was all just preparation. After the kickoff/tipping point, it's all just picking up the pieces and strategizing your next move down the field.

ALEX FROM TARGET AND MERIDITH FROM . . . DIGITOUR?

It was 9 P.M. on a cold November night. Chris and I were settled on the couch, intent on catching up with *The Real Housewives of Beverly Hills*, and combing through social media.

Believe me when I say our relaxation was well earned. We had just finished the Jack & Jack headline tour, followed by a sold-out night at Citi Field with DigiFest NYC. Twelve thousand, five hundred fans; one hundred social media stars—including Fifth Harmony; and a feature on the front page of *The New York Times*. DigiTour was really starting to grow and we were pulling double duty with a tiny team.

#MeridithFromDigiTour with #AlexFromTarget

In Frisco, Texas, a quiet suburb of Dallas just over fifteen hundred miles from our comfy couch in L.A., a storm was brewing. A storm that, within hours, would drastically change the life of an average teenage boy and, in doing so, make an indelible mark on social media as we know it.

Sixteen-year-old Alex LaBeouf was working his Sunday shift as a checkout boy at Target when a customer snapped a candid photo of him bagging groceries. She posted it on her Twitter account. Within hours, a furor had erupted on social media. By the following morning, Alex, the unassuming, anonymous teenager who bagged your laundry detergent, had become Alex From Target.

Lucky for us, we got to watch the entire episode unfold.

At the time, Chris was running our Twitter account. Not only was I a perpetual fourteen-year-old girl, apparently so was my husband's inner voice. Almost every post he wrote received its share of "literally me" in the comments. YouTuber Shane Dawson asked me once, "What gay assistant do you have running the account?" So when the first waves of Alex From Target began to ripple the otherwise placid social-media plane that night, Chris was one of the first ones to pick up on it.

"Hey, check this out," he said. "This kid in Texas who works at Target is trending!" He handed me the phone so I could have a look. I could tell from the info included on the tweet some of what was going on. A Directioner fan account had tweeted about how this teen from Target was "the best-looking guy in the world." (Directioners is the name we give to the massive social media following of British boy band One Direction, who also happen to comprise a large portion of DigiTour's audience.)

Did I mention they were enthusiastic? Every tweet glowed with the effusive teen energy I can't get enough of, and suddenly, the fourteen-year-old in me lit up—I needed to know more! My imagination ran wild with the same frenzy that was setting the social media world ablaze. Who is this guy? What does he do? And—finally—where can I see this picture?

"Pic please!" I shouted. There he was, a kid with floppy, sandy-colored hair, wearing a red T-shirt and loading a bag with somebody's purchases. The only info we had on him came from his name tag, which bore the Target logo and his name: Alex. "Hmm, okay, Alex From Target," I said, unaware that by the following morning, that's how he'd be known to the world.

Chris went on Photoshop and edited a photo of Alex From Target onstage at a DigiTour event. He tweeted the photo to a few hundred thousand DigiTour followers and, within minutes, #AlexFromTargetOnDigiTour became the number-two trend on social media, just under #AlexFromTarget.

"This is nuts!" I said to Chris, but neither of us was surprised. This is the way we'd always done things. Our tried-and-true approach to making it in social media is to: 1) Stay plugged in constantly; 2) Jump in while it's still getting hot; 3) Listen like crazy. It's all about the fans and no one else. The next day Ellen DeGeneres called Alex, and so did we.

Sudden viral fame could not have happened to a more unsuspecting kid. Alex From Target was—and still is—shy. If the Directioner fandom had chosen a song from their namesake boy band to fuel the soundtrack to November 2, 2014, it would have been "What Makes You Beautiful." Perhaps most ironic is how *not* active he was on social media. Prior to his overnight ride to social stardom he had around a hundred followers on Twitter. In a little over a month, as he was being flown to L.A. to be featured on *Ellen* and interviewed by *The Huffington Post* and *Time*, that number soared to three hundred thousand.

Despite not being as plugged in to the social media that brought him to fame, he was familiar with DigiTour, and more than willing to hear what we had to say. We brought him to L.A. and like many social stars we work with, at our first meeting he was shy, unsuspecting, and clearly enjoying this ride of craziness. I gave him my usual warm welcome and invited him to sit in the conference room. "Coffee? Tea?" I asked.

"No, don't worry about it; I'm good, I don't want to be a bother," he said with a smile.

"Okay," I said. "If you were to join us on DigiTour, what do you think you want to do onstage?"

His eyes grew big and I could tell he was nervous. "Ahhh . . . I don't know."

"Do you dance?" No. "Sing?" No. "Act?" No. "No problem."

This was some of my favorite talent to work with because it required a little extra creativity. "How do you feel about fan fiction?" I asked.

He responded with a shy laugh.

"You read it all the time, don't you?" He laughed again.

"I mean, I don't read it but I know what it is. . . ." Clearly he knew Wattpad could get a little heavy on the make-out sessions.

"Well, what if we find a PG fan fic about you and have you read it to the audience like story time, *Masterpiece Theatre* . . . how funny and fun?" I tried to gauge his reaction; if he thought I'd forgotten to take my meds that morning, I could pivot and tell him I was joking the whole time.

"That's cool," he said, nonchalantly. "I could do that."

Four weeks later, Fan Fic Story Time with Alex From Target was officially part of the run of show and Alex was in Long Island with me, my husband, six other talent, a crew of another six, and one thousand teen girls all screaming at the tops of their lungs.

I've always loved a first show. The excitement brings me back to my own fangirl teen days, adrenaline rush and all. For someone like Alex, who wasn't yet accustomed to what to expect, the whole experience was overwhelming. When we drove into the venue, girls ran up to the bus, banging on the windows and doors, tipping us from side to side. They blocked the street so we couldn't move and wouldn't relent until we finally agreed to roll down the window for a few selfies. The perpetual teen I am, I believe effort that good deserves a reward. Alex, on the other hand, looked shell-shocked.

"You all right?" I asked him.

"Is it always like this?" he asked.

"No. Sometimes the bus tips over." His eyes widened. "I'm kidding!"

The crowd was roaring as the emcee pumped Top 40 pop music through the venue. The meet & greet of three hundred hysterical fans had just come to a close and the general admission ticket holders were rushing in. Fans had been waiting outside in the freezing cold for hours, but it didn't faze them one bit, because in minutes they were going to meet their internet boyfriends. The room flooded with high-pitched squeals and bright handmade poster boards bearing DIGI in glitter and the names of the stars, including ALEX.

Right before the show started, I gave our talent a pep talk. "Phones down, phones down! Okay, guys, it's our first show! I know this feels weird, and those are *real* people out there, but they're all here for *you*. They don't care if you mess up or fall or anything, they just want to see you be you. It's sold out, it's going to be great, and make sure you take a few selfies while you're out there because you're going to look like a rock star."

It was a huge coup to get any of our stars to focus for five consecutive minutes. "Okay, how do you feel?" They all shouted "Good" in unison and I gave a series of hugs and high-fives and then let everyone retreat to their green room for some rest (aka more selfies and some live broadcasting), while I went to my perch side stage on top of an amp.

Finally, the show began. The lights dimmed and the screams grew deafening. Thousands of girls were pushed up to the barricades in front of the stage, squished together so tightly that they moved as one solid mass, with hardly enough room to hold up their phones to film. The emcee took the stage like a ringmaster at the circus, shouting, "Who's ready for DigiTour!?" The screams hit a new level of loud and you could feel the sound vibrating off the floor. I spotted several girls with shiny tearstains on their perfectly contoured cheeks (thanks to YouTube for their makeup perfection!). From the steady din of high-pitched screams, you could hear "I love you!" or "He's so hot!"

We had several segments unfold: a music act, a live challenge, and some video on the big screens. Halfway through the show, I got a text from one of our DigiTour team members. "I think Alex is missing." My first thought was *Don't panic.* My second: *Come to think of it, I haven't seen Alex since the meet & greet.* Then my first thought flew out the window and I began to panic. A full-on *Home Alone* montage spun my imagination out of control. Where could he be? Was he locked outside? It was two degrees out. I was picturing an icicle wearing a red Target shirt.

The scenarios in my mind began to darken. Did he get kidnapped by a mob of fans? They're stronger than they look, and ridiculously clever. I traipsed through the tangle of wires and cables that lined the backstage landscape in my four-inch heels. The manhunt was on. I checked every corner, room, and doorway backstage. Nothing. I asked every crew member I encountered. Negative. I peeked through the frosty stage door. Empty. I squinted through the crack that gave me a glimpse of the audience. Thousands of screaming teenagers, but no Alex. Finally, as I was about to call the police, I spotted him, timidly perched on a couch in the farthest corner of the green-room basement.

"Alex! You're okay!" I said, trying not to show how desperate I was.

"I'm okay," he said bashfully.

"Your segment is coming up. Are you going onstage?"

"I don't remember what to do."

He wasn't lost, frostbitten, or kidnapped. Just a little stage fright is all.

"Alex, I know this is weird. But that's okay. Those screams out there? Yeah, those are for you. You can't let them down. These fans bought tickets and have been waiting for you to come out onstage. And I don't know if you ever met a girl from Long Island, but . . ." His blank expression told me my joke had fallen flat; he didn't get it.

As terrifying as this was for shy Alex, I think he realized that letting down a thousand screaming girls was even scarier. I saw him swallow hard and steel himself. "Pretend you're just shooting content in your room," I offered.

"Um, I don't know what that means."

"Oh. Right. Duh. Well . . . pretend you're just bagging groceries." That got him to laugh and I saw him start to relax. "Don't worry about it. You'll be fine. I promise you. Once those girls hear you start they'll scream so loud no one will hear anything anyway." I giggled, and got another smile in return.

In that moment, I was Mom. Not his mother but just someone that had their stuff together, basically, which helped Alex to get his together. "Alright Alex, it's time. Let's go." I led him up to the side stage. Once he hit the stage, he'd be fine. I knew this because I'd seen it before, many, many times. I just needed to make sure he didn't flee.

The emcee announced, "Okay, guys, up next we have a very special surprise . . . who knows ALEX FROM TARGET?" The bellow of screams meant there wasn't a doubt in the house. "Well," said the emcee, "he thought it might be fun to scroll through Wattpad with you and have a little story time!"

In that moment some of the audience may have actually gone through puberty. Looks of shock and disbelief swept over the crowd. Was this really happening? Is it really him? A massive, simultaneous OMG was the general response.

Alex shyly stepped onto the stage. The light hit him in the face and his hand shot up to cover his eyes. It was one of the cutest and most genuine moments I'd ever seen onstage. I was on the side wing like a stage mom, smiling and offering as much physical encouragement as I could since he couldn't hear anything but the audience screaming. I motioned for him to put his hand down and then gave him my biggest "You're going to do great!" smile, even though—between you and me—I was a bit nervous for him. What if he forgot to open the "fan fic" prop with the printed-out story? (Side note: the story had actually been written by me, since Wattpad Alex From Target fan fics at the time were all way too dirty to read aloud at DigiTour.)

All my fears were dispelled as Alex opened the book. He held the mic to his lips, looked down, and said in a feeble voice, "Hi." The audience roared in delight. Then he began to read. "I was working that day. I pulled on my red T-shirt, ran my fingers through my hair, and quickly checked in. I was going to be on register two. Out of the corner of my eye was the most beautiful girl I had ever seen. . . ."

"Oooooo," the audience cooed, as though it were one big campfire story. Alex went on to read a story in which he asked a girl on the other side of the checkout counter to go out with him. He grabbed her phone and put his number in it, a line which earned an "Ahhhh," from the audience. At the end, they went out together and even shared a kiss. Cringey? Maybe, but for this audience it was pure fantasy perfection.

After that, Alex had no problem taking the stage and embracing the role he played in all of this. He read his Fireside Fan Fic for twenty-three more shows, always with a shy side smile, and he even got down in the dance-off segments by doing the worm.

Being a Selfie Made CEO sometimes means giving throngs of screaming young girls exactly what they want before they even know they want it. And sometimes it means being Mom to the most famous face of the latest news cycle. The only constants in my job are my walkie-talkie, two smartphones, and four-inch heels.

TRYING TO GO VIRAL

People can tell when you're trying too hard, and your digital-native peers can sniff out your desperation faster than they can sniff out an electric socket to plug their phone into. Alex was a totally unsuspecting person, who launched an online brand without really trying. Who was responsible for Alex's sudden fame? It certainly wasn't Alex himself (or his mother, for giving him those good hair genes). It wasn't the girl who snapped the photo at Target, either. It was the Directioner on Twitter, with the fourteen thousand followers. She lit a match, whose spark caught the attention of her very engaged followers, who then passed along the message to everyone they knew, thereby setting the entire internet ablaze.

With that said, you can see how every viral sensation had a tipping point. There are lots of tipping points, but usually people don't know what to do with them. Being prepared for it to happen can mean the difference between a few dozen new followers and a headlining spot on DigiTour.

WHAT IS CLICKBAIT?

"You're never going to believe this."

"See what happens next!"

My (least) favorite clickbaits are the ones that say, "These celebs died too soon," and then the picture is of an actor who's very much alive. They get me every time.

Clickbait can seemingly be a way to go viral. It usually utilizes a misleading title that piques a viewer's interest.

Some social stars have gone with this approach. They'll title a post something like, "i got arrested," or "making out with my ex." Something like that would make a fan click for sure!

Now, if you actually got arrested, and posted about what happened, that's fine. Not fine that you got arrested, that sounds terrible, but it's fine to say what happened in your title.

The big no-no is mistitling something so someone gets excited to see what your title suggests and then having video content that is totally unrelated. In that case, while you may get the view, you will lose some followers/subscribers. I've seen it happen. You can't build a house out of fake bricks, and you can't build your following with fake posts.

Clickbait can backfire in a big way. Like when Logan Paul posted the now much-criticized video of Japan's suicide forest titled "We Found a Dead Body . . ." This title was shocking and led millions of his fans to click. The

Me, Blake Gray, and Mark Thomas at PTTOW! Sessions NYC schooling some peeps on social media PTTOW!

disturbing content has since been removed from YouTube and many have spoken out against Paul. The title wasn't fake, but this is still an example of clickbait gone bad, as Logan took a sad and controversial subject like suicide and exploited it for views. Some things shouldn't be used for clicks. There's no hard-and-fast rule; just try to grab people's attention without offending an entire country.

Final verdict on clickbait? Definitely use captivating and enticing titles and thumbnails for your content, but make sure you deliver what you promise. Otherwise, you'll have some unhappy viewers, and in the long run it only hurts you.

INSTA MODELS

Okay, you've seen the type of social influencers who opt to rely on their good looks as their hook. This is not uncommon, and it's a type that has always existed in teen fandoms, since before the internet was even a thing. The "teen dream," the perfect boyfriend or girlfriend. They post captions like: "I need a girlfriend rn" and "shut up and kiss me," or "I just want someone to go to the movies with me . . ."

Pros: this can help you get likes and attention quickly.

Cons: this doesn't last forever. Trevor Moran told me, "Okay, be attractive, but don't rely on it. Do something you can turn to as an actual career."

Me (center) at DigiTour Winter 2016 with (from left to right) Mark Thomas, Weston Koury, Nathan Triska, Blake Gray, Zach Clayton, and Baby Ariel

This can also lead you to become a running joke among other social talent. Let's be honest: while there is an audience for this kind of content, it also rubs a lot of other people the wrong way. It can be polarizing. And as Trevor pointed out, it doesn't always last. There is a way to play off the excitement of your audience and provide good pictures that are certain to make the heart flutter, but at the very least use a more subtle, authentic caption.

It is all subjective, but if you go too far with playing off the "boyfriend fantasy," you may make everyone cringe, including your fans! Also, if your fans are thirteen and fourteen, by the time you hit eighteen it gets a little creepy. Less can be more.

CHALLENGES/VIDEO TAGS WITH BLAKE GRAY

Video tags originated on YouTube. Popular YouTubers would theme a video, and then the theme would catch on and become a tag.

For example: #boyfrienddoesmymakeup, #drawmylife, #readinghatecomments, and #firsttime. YouTube is the number-two most popular search engine in the world. If you use a hot hashtag, there's the potential for your video tag to pop up when people search for it.

You don't really hear people use the term "video tag" much anymore. Once other platforms started making good use of video content, video tags started morphing into challenges.

For example: #dontjudgemechallenge, #cinnamonchallenge, or the one that started it all, #icebucketchallenge.

Popular challenges are a proven and reliably searched type of content, and they're viewed by millions of fans. Just like the trending tags and challenges on other platforms, creating your version and tagging it with the corresponding hashtags gets you in the mix.

Social media superstar Blake Gray used a challenge to change his path to social stardom forever!

Blake Gray's tipping point was the #dontjudgemechallenge. The requirements were fairly simple—make a video of yourself looking super-unattractive. For Blake, this was no small task as he's extremely handsome. But with a Sharpie goatee, tape on his nose, and a unibrow, he made his mark.

"I had ten thousand followers on Instagram at the time, mostly from #f4f (follow for follow) and posting good pics, Blake explained. I thought it was cool and definitely wanted to get bigger. I saw the #dontjudgemechallenge before it was really big. There were maybe five hundred other people who had done it by the time I posted mine on Instagram. The next day my vid went viral. I grew eighty thousand followers in one day. People at school kept saying to me, 'Wow I'm seeing you everywhere.'"

The key point to Blake's story? He jumped on the challenge "before it was really big." That's kinda the whole point. If you're jumping on the bandwagon after something has been posted to death, don't expect a Blake Gray outcome.

I asked Blake to break down his tips for jumping on a challenge or trend:

1: Be different. Show your personality. "I used a different song than everyone else was. It made me stand out."

2: Be on it early! Timing is important—don't wait until your grandparents already posted theirs.

3: Be creative. Being first isn't an excuse for bad quality. Put time and thought into it!

COVER SONGS

For some musicians, posting remixes and covers has the same effect as a challenge. In the boom of early YouTube, when DigiTour was just starting out, one of the most popular category of YouTuber was cover artist: there were Kurt Hugo Schneider, Alex Goot, and Madilyn Bailey, just to name a few.

Cover artists would anxiously await Taylor Swift's or Justin Bieber's announcement for their next single and sometimes would burn the midnight oil to stay up and be the first uploaded cover, knowing that as soon as the song was announced and released, fans would be searching for it like crazy.

This tactic yielded *millions* of views for some cover artists, who turned those views into legions of their own fans. It also resulted in quite a bit of money being generated. Many of the cover artists on YouTube made their living from both the ad revenue on their channel and by selling their covers on iTunes.

Depending on how old you are, you may or may not remember the cover artist duo Karmin. They uploaded a cover of Chris Brown's "Look at Me Now" in 2011 that now has over 100 million views.

In the initial days following the upload of that cover, Karmin was in the middle of one of the biggest-ever bidding wars between record labels. Every major record label tried to ink the group. They ended up signing to Epic Records with L. A. Reid at the helm.

The viral success of their cover never ended up translating into more mainstream success for the duo. But their unique spin on a popular song, mixed with the power of the internet, yielded one of the most talked-about early YouTube moments.

Similarly, there was a major boom of a cappella YouTubers and YouTube remixers. If a song is resonating in pop culture, you can bet the internet is abuzz with remixing or mixing it up and sharing it like crazy.

The cover as a means to promote your original music and build socials remains a reliable method of getting noticed. The new wave of talent has turned less to YouTube to produce full music videos and more to other platforms, like Instagram and Musical.ly. Whatever platform you're using, try to get to the cover first, and remember to tag it with as many versions of the original artist's name and the name of the song as you can think of. You want your song to come up early in searches for it.

Bryce Xavier Wants To Do It All

Big ambitions have paid off for Bryce Xavier, one of the most multitalented Selfie Made stars! Whether he's playing violin with the Disney Orchestra, acting in numerous TV shows, choreographing for Will.i.Am, or modeling for the biggest clothing brands, Bryce is living the dream. But none of that would've been possible without his fan base (known as the #Bees) that he grew on social media! Bryce is the textbook definition of being #SelfieMade.

How did you get started?

I was an actor and wanted to find a way to get my content directly out to people. Instagram is where I started, and I had about 3,000 followers as an actor. Then I got into Musical.ly and started with zero followers and built it up quick. I'd do promotions on Instagram and drive people to Musical.ly from there. Four months in, I got crowned. Musical.ly started the fire, and my job as a creator is to keep the fire burning.

What was your tipping point?

My content was different, so it stood out and helped me get featured. I'd take challenges from Instagram and YouTube, like dancing challenges, and I'd do them on Musical.ly. Once I got featured, I started getting more and more features, and people kept seeing my face everywhere.

What's the best advice you can give to someone just starting out?

Try new things, even things you're not good at. It shows a lot of personality. And get good lighting. People want to see your face.

Photo courtesy of Jhanna Shaghag

What does being an influencer mean to you?

It's a really big job. Anything I say on social media can be misconstrued and affect people's lives in major ways. It's a big deal to me to only promote things I believe in. I don't want to break my followers' trust in me.

How do you handle hate?

I focus on positivity, and I don't throw hate around on social. Promote positivity and you'll get it back. Usually. I got a lot of backlash when I defended a friend once, which was hard. Any hate comments I get I reply with something nice, and then usually I'll get a DM back saying thank you.

How would you describe your relationship to your audience?

No matter what, they tell me how they feel. About everything. I always reply back. I share things with them that I would share with family and close friends. Doing IRL events like DigiTour is important because it's one of the only times I can meet my followers in person, which is just as important to me as it is to them.

What does being #selfiemade mean to you?

My socials gave me the opportunity to do what I've always wanted to do: act. Rather than waiting for Hollywood to notice me, I went out and made my own way. Social media gives us these opportunities, but you still have to put the work in to make them happen.

What are your goals now?

I want to get to one million followers on Instagram, and be on 3 magazine covers. I know that's super specific and maybe strange, but I try to keep my goals achievable. Once I get to my goals, I'll set new goals.

Selfie Made Mode:

- ▷ You can't control what will go viral, but you can help your chances.
- ▷ Think outside the box. Figure out what makes you unique, and run with it!
- ▷ Focus your content. Keep your goals in mind.

Influencers

STAN definition: stan

stan/

informal

noun

An overzealous or obsessive fan of a person, place or thing.

Example: "He has millions of stans who are obsessed with him and call him a rap god."

verb

To be an overzealous or obsessive fan of a particular person, place, or thing.

Example: "Y'all know I stan for Max & Harvey, so I was excited to see them at DigiTour!"

Synonyms

Super Fan, First Fan, Family

While there's no way to know what will go viral next, there *are* ways you can stack the odds in your favor. *Influence* is the name of the game, and it is influencers who are the star players.

Influencers are relatable storytellers who are welcoming and comforting to people who need a community.

Influencers attract and control a *lot* of eyeballs. They are the trusted voices who set trends and curate popular taste. A weight-loss tea or lip kit can sell millions of units through the placement in certain talents' videos/posts. The same concept applies to recommending new music, fashion, movies, and other channels/pages to follow.

When I was fifteen, my CD collection was hugely valuable, not only because it cost a lot to put together, but also because it represented my taste in music, my memories, and my soundtrack. If you had an awesome CD collection, your house would probably be a preferred destination for a hangout. Today you would call it aux cord privileges. Whoever gets the cord in the car to play DJ usually has the best taste in music, and they don't have to lug around ten pounds of CDs with them anymore.

Today, music and video content is plentiful because of the internet. You don't even need to be a paying subscriber on Spotify or Pandora to stream your favorite music; you can listen to ads and let the brands pay for you. You can listen to music playlists on YouTube vids, TV shows, or movies . . . the point is that there is more than you can actually consume. What you need is more time . . . or, someone who can help you decide what music is worth spending your time on.

Influencers are the de facto kings and queens of the aux cord privileges. They not only tell you what new music is worth listening to but so much more: movies, fashion, and products. They cut through the noise and help you decide because you already know you like what they like and you trust them; therefore they can curate for you.

The role influencers play is a powerful one. Key social talent specifically hold the power to activate and influence a large number of people. That is why talent on social are often called influencers in the first place. When talking about influence, you can't ignore the actual influencers. They are called this for a very deserving reason!

What do influencers have to do with going viral? Well, catching the attention of people and accounts who are the gatekeepers of news, gossip, trends, and all things cool can *help* something go viral, wouldn't you say? If you love Hayes Grier, and he starts posting links to RiceGum's new video, saying he's the most hilarious new YouTuber, that probably will lead you to click and check him out.

For RiceGum, this is exactly what happened. RiceGum already had his tipping point after posting his first *These Kids Must Be Stopped* video, about the Musical.ly phenomenon. Not only did he react to fans, but other influencers loved him and they were not quiet about it. An endorsement from Hayes Grier and many other influencers sent him into the stratosphere.

FANDOMS

Often, stans are the ones breaking news, even before Just Jared or Perez Hilton get to it (or for you social fans, Messy Monday or Muser Shaderoom).

Stans do not live in social exile. They congregate, across all different social platforms, with other stans. These congregations are called fandoms.

If a Directioner fandom could get Alex From Target to go viral, why can't the same happen to you? You should get to know your way around the eclectic (and cliquey) pop fandom armies. You have Directioners, Swifties, Harmonizers, and of course, Beliebers. Favorite movies have fandoms (like *The Hunger Games*), and movie stars (like Jennifer Lawrence), and books (I'm going to use *The Hunger Games* as an example again because I have this theme going now and I'm sticking with it), and of course all your social media favs have their own fandoms.

Fandom culture is comprised of extreme enthusiasts who have detailed and thoughtful discussions about their influencer. They make fan art and edits, find out and spread little-known facts and info, and identify with the characteristics of the fandom. The most obvious questions are: what are your interests, and what are the corresponding fandoms?

Even if your interests have nothing to do with your social brand, it is worth looking into those fandoms (and also worth looking into why your brand isn't based on your interests). If you like comic book movies, go find a fandom for your favorite superhero. If you love John Green or Anna Todd novels, go see what their fandoms are talking about!

How do you get on the inside with a fandom? It can be as simple as reaching out to other known fans. Usually around certain releases (new music, new movies, new books, or promotions with their fav social talent) there is more excitement surrounding influencers. They even have group activities. This could come in the form of official or unofficial Twitter Parties, or jumping into fan live broadcasts.

Once you have your foot in the fan door then you can get to know who ranks high on the totem pole. Some fan accounts have thirty- to fifty thousand of their *own* highly engaged followers. Before the internet, stars had fan clubs that would send out signed headshots and other memorabilia through a mailing list. Now these virtual fan clubs band together to get something trending or to get noticed and get the ultimate digital autograph: a follow or DM.

You may be asking: why are we talking about fandoms when I'm still working on the fans? *Because fandoms hold a lot of power.* They're accessible in a way the actual star can't always be.

Let's put it this way. If you have three million followers, you can't possibly interact with all of them in a meaningful way. But if you were going to connect with as many as you could, the fans who devote the time to run fan accounts for you are going to get priority. And in a community of a bunch of stans, the stan with the most direct access to the star is the leader of the pack.

The Directioner account that helped Alex From Target turned fourteen thousand superfans into an unpaid marketing team that broke the internet. These fan accounts carry their own influence, and having a direct line to them is essential to a star trying to connect with his or her community.

If you're able to get friendly with these highly engaged accounts, they can become extremely helpful in promoting your channel, *when* and *if* you can get them interested. Do you see the way I italicized *when* and *if* there? That's because I didn't say it was going to be easy, and I'm not saying you should expect these fandoms to see your brand the way you want them to. It will take a genuine commitment on your part, along with a little luck (but much less luck than you'd need to go viral).

Start right now. Do the work. Give yourself a crash course on at least one fandom that seems to align with your content. Join their community, engage with it, and figure out who the influence gatekeepers are.

CONVERSATE LIKE A PRO

You want to connect with a fandom, and start making friends and followers on the internet. Great! What are you going to talk to them about? What do you have to say? How do you get in the conversation? It starts by *following the conversation*.

My mom used to tell me to read all the headlines in the newspaper, every day. "You never want someone to ask you about a current event and be clueless about what they're talking about," she would say. And I believed her! Now we have news sites that aggregate the headlines for you, so you don't even have to get newspaper ink all over your hands in order to get this done. Or even easier, just scroll through Twitter.

What Mom said is a lot truer now than it ever was. Being clued in to pop culture is the only way to engage with it. If you want to be a part of pop culture, you have to follow it. Imagine being asked what #howboutdah or wyd means and having no idea? How embarrassing! If you want your finger on the pulse, you need to stick it in a socket (aka plug in).

If you know what everyone is talking about, then you automatically have something to say. Start by asking questions; see what people think. In fact, lesson for life, if you're ever hanging out with someone, either online or IRL, and you don't know what to say, ask a question.

Number-one no-no when interacting with fandom accounts: don't be cheesy. No oversell. Don't let Siwanators or Angels know that *Selfie Made* sent you on a research mission. Just play it cool; engage with whatever conversation they're having. Respect your place as a newcomer in their group, and see where it leads you.

WHO TO FOLLOW

If you're not sure what influencers you like, or what fandoms are right for you, that's okay. To start out, just follow the most talked about influencers. In fact, I'll make it easier for you. Whenever you see the name of a social media star in this book, follow them on your platform of choice.

Doing this will give you a really strong sense of who is out there really putting in the effort and making it work. And you'll see that they're all people, just like you! None of them are superhumans. No special powers. Yes, lots of dreamy eyes and wavy hair, but those aren't superpowers! When you check out the influencers I talked to for this book, you'll see that some of them will really click with you, and others you might not really care for. That's okay; you can unfollow and follow new people! That's what's so great about social media; you can find exactly where you fit in.

Maybe you're a bit of a nerd like me and want even more ways to research what's trending. For you, check out Tubefilter.com. It's an online video trade publication that will keep you up to date on all the social media headlines. Then you can go to DigiTour's website (thedigitour.com) and see who we are featuring, or VidCon to see who the conference features on their main stage.

Or, if you have a taste for the slightly more salacious, follow @MessyMonday (the TMZ of social) and see who they're talking about today. Once you have a few names the rest is easy. Creators follow other creators. There's no shortage of beef and drama and often you can let a real-time reality show unfold on your feed as creators call each other out, date each other, break up, and, hopefully, make up! Congratulations, you're in the social media circle.

THE KEY TO SUCCESS IN ONE SECOND!

Okay, that headline was a lie to get you to keep reading. Here's what I really wanted to make sure you read:

THINK BEFORE POSTING.

The good thing about being Gen Z is you get to connect with the entire world.

The bad thing? Once you publish something, even a Snap, it's out there forever. Others will screenshot and screen record it and share it. There are no do-overs here. #FR

👍 TOP POP FANDOMS

Justin Bieber—Beliebers

Taylor Swift—Swifties

One Direction—Directioners

Selena Gomez—Selenators

Beyoncé—Beyhive

Ariana Grande—Arianators

Fifth Harmony—Harmonizers

Demi Lovato—Lovatics

👍 SOCIAL STAR FANDOMS

Loren Gray—Angels

Jojo Siwa—Siwanators

Baby Ariel—Babies

James Charles—Sisters

Miranda Sings—Mirfandas

MEME ACCOUNTS

A meme is a humorous image, video, piece of text, etc., that is copied (often with slight variations) and spread rapidly by internet users. Meme accounts are dedicated to spreading humorous content.

Some influencers got their start by sharing funny pop culture commentary in meme form. Whether it's a Kim Kardashian crying meme, or Kermit sipping tea, an easy way to break ice and recruit internet friends is to pump out supershareable content.

There is nothing the internet loves more than a good meme. Did you know The Gabbie Show, Joanne the Scammer, and Jack Baran all started as meme accounts before they transitioned into personalities? This tactic can be employed by any uber-creative influencer in training.

If you have the comic chops, you can use your sharp wit and humor to accumulate an initial following, which you can slowly but surely transition into more personal non-memes, in order to broaden your account.

First things first: get to know the popular accounts. Which accounts speak to your sense of humor? What do they have in common/what do they do differently? What are they not doing that you could bring into the mix? You need to know what your competition is doing and make sure you're staying on top of trends.

If a popular meme account were to repost your content and tag you, it could yield a big boost in your social media following. They tend to repost the memes that get the most attention . . . but tagging an account is a great way to get their attention. You can also try DM (direct messaging) or sending to a business email address if they have one in their bio. Watermarking the meme/image with your Instagram handle is a good idea to make sure you get credit if your work is used. A lot of big accounts may not bother crediting you otherwise.

Q&A with Ceci Allison, who runs M3SSY M0nday Instagram

The TMZ of social media, Messy Monday spills all the tea all over Twitter and Insta multiple times per day. If you get shaded on his accounts, chances are he's sparking a buzzing conversation on you. He uncovers all the gossip and gets insider tips: who's dating who, who's fighting with who, and the general happenings in the internet world.

Top five tips for posting content?

1. Post something people will have to put an opinion on; people love expressing their opinion.
2. Don't keep posting about one topic; post things that everyone will be interested in so you can have multiple follower types.
3. Don't be biased!
4. Try adding humor; people love to laugh.
5. Post popular content.

How did you get started?

I started off as a confessions page at first, but then I changed into a celebrity-update page.

What inspired you to start Messy Monday?

I've always been interested in celebrity news. I used to tell my friends and family what was new in the celebrity world. So I took my interests and turned it into an Instagram page.

What was the moment you started to grow/get big?

As I continued to post, people started finding interest in my page and started telling their friends about my page. The moment that my page started to grow was when big influencers started finding interest as well.

How important is it to stay active?

It's incredibly important to stay active. If you aren't active, people start to think that you aren't running your account anymore. It also shows loss of interest.

How does someone catch your attention so you talk about them?

The way I choose who to post about is by seeing if they trigger a crowd. People love showing their reactions in situations and if it's a huge deal, then people will respond to it.

Advice you'd give someone starting out?

Never give up. Yes, it's difficult to gain and become successful, but all you need is time and patience.

NEWS OUTLETS WITH MUSCLE

Just like I told that Condé Nast investor, if you're under the age of twenty-five, you're probably not reading magazines. Or at least the old paper version you can buy when you check out at the supermarket. Your news is in your social feed. The new magazine is the Twitter, Insta, or Snap of one of your fav creators.

If this is you, then your "celeb" gossip comes from a site like Messy Monday, Muser Shaderoom, or Superfame.

These accounts are the equivalent of *Us Weekly* or TMZ. They're not covering Justin Bieber or Ed Sheeran but instead Annie LeBlanc and Hayden Summeral, Bhad Bhabie, Malu, or Tana Mongeau. Scroll through and see who's dating who, who did what when going live last night, who's shading who, and so on.

To be mentioned or noticed by one of these outlets has its pros and cons, but most influencers generally see it as an important part of getting bigger. The same way Kylie Jenner may complain about being on the cover of the tabloids, it's also that coverage that makes her a superstar. Same concept with these social outlets.

Selfie Made Mode:

▶ Know your influencers; respect their fandoms.

▶ Engage. Become part of the conversation. Ask questions!

▶ Not sure who to follow? Start with every name mentioned in this book!

Get
Featured

Social media platforms would love nothing more than for you to be ultrasuccessful with them. If you develop a fan base, you are growing their user base. With that in mind, some platforms have designed a way to help break you through to a world of future fans: the *oh so* coveted features.

For most of the social stars I know who have a "going viral" story, getting featured was the key factor in transitioning from average user to above-average influencer. Understanding the power of getting featured, along with some tricks to increase your odds, may give you the edge you need to go viral.

Traditional talent looks toward radio, TV talk shows, or substantial write-ups/photo spreads in magazines or print media to promote themselves and their projects. However, this is changing, and no one understands this more than social media stars. Some of the talent we work with at DigiTour will ask me about the reach well-known magazines have before agreeing to do an interview. If their own following is larger online than that of the publication, it actually does more for the outlet than the talent, as far as exposure and follower growth.

Today's internet-bred talent focus on getting featured on platforms that control population-sized audiences of hundreds of millions, like Musical.ly (100M+) and Instagram (700M+). Being featured by one of these popular platforms can lead to tens of thousands of new followers, or in some cases, millions!

YouTube and Instagram may have the largest audiences, but smaller and newer platforms, like Musical.ly, were the ones helping the most new talent in the last twenty-four months. Features on YouNow have also helped promote a new wave of talent. Understanding how newer platforms like these select talent to be featured can help you understand what you should focus on when shooting/

Me at Musical.ly HQ in Santa Monica

uploading content. Those are the platforms that *need* more talent and more activity. If you're spending time creating content on their app, your chances of getting featured grow exponentially. We'll get further into this in the next chapter.

(Side note: Danielle Cohn told me that one of these platforms supporting new talent is not a new platform at all, but the once photo-collage-only app Flipagram. It's having a resurgence with younger audiences and there are now Flipagram stars. While this is a new concept, it may be a good place to invest some time and energy.)

YouNow has editor's picks. Musical.ly tends to select videos out of their hashtags and conversations, giving the creator more opportunities to get noticed. If you opt to post non-lip-syncing content (despite that being the content the app is most known for), your chances of a feature are increased. Actual singing, dancing, or comedy skits/sketches are getting more love and attention in the features department. That's how a new app like Musical.ly can diversify and grow.

For Lauren Godwin, her very first Musical.ly was featured the day after she posted. That propelled her into gaining five thousand new followers per day. Nathan Triska climbed the hashtag ladder on YouNow and found his tipping point, which gave him the boost he needed to turn his hobby into a career.

There's no magic way to get featured on a platform, but the trick is to understand which ones *do* get featured, and how they work.

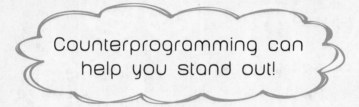
Counterprogramming can help you stand out!

Danielle Cohn

Musical.ly Made Me a Star!

Danielle Cohn, who boasts nearly eight million fans, grew her fan base in just eighteen months. While some may think it was her viral music video for her song "Marilyn Monroe," it was actually Musical.ly and a string of features that helped her explode in record time. I asked her a few questions to better understand what her experience was like:

How did you get started?

I saw the #dontjudgemechallenge on Instagram. I didn't understand how people were starting and stopping the video until I discovered it was with an app called Musical.ly. I joined it and really liked it. After one or two months I was featured. I started posting every other day and after the feature I started gaining ten thousand to thirty thousand fans per day! It was not long after that I was getting featured every week. Six months after that I hit a million followers, and then I hit four million. At that point someone reached out to me and asked if I wanted to make a song. He said if we do it, we want it to go viral. I didn't love the song, but it did go viral and got ten million views on YouTube. After "Marilyn Monroe" came out my following grew to eight million.

What was the response to the song going viral?

It was fifty-fifty—a lot of positive but also a lot of negative.

How do you deal with the hate?

I personally don't care.

If someone was to go viral tomorrow, what advice would you give them to maximize that experience?

Don't change—a lot of people change when they get famous, but that makes people not want to work with them because they're bragging all the time. Also, be strong, because you will get a lot of hate.

How do you make money?

Live.ly: the first time someone gave me a gift (panda) I didn't know what it was. I realized when I cashed it out. It was a hundred dollars!

Brand deals: I was one of the new Art Class designers for a collection at Target.

Tips for getting featured on Musical.ly?

- Use hashtags! It's the best way to get noticed. Musical.ly goes through those to select for features.
- Good lighting. Invest in a ring light!
- Post a lot per day. Based on the number of likes you get per day you can get on the leaderboard. So while on some platforms you may only want to post once per day, on Musical.ly it's the more, the merrier.

INSTAGRAM

While there are things that can be done to increase your odds of being featured on their popular/explore page, based on the info Instagram provides on this subject, it's all quite vague and random-based (aka algorithmic).

The way Instagram outlines their selection process is based on the individual user and who they follow and the posts they like. Basically, the videos selected on your explore page are different than those on mine. Instagram curates these pages and creates an explore page based on what they think you may like.

There are a few tips to improving your chances but it is still an at-random process.

♥ Age of your account: should be at least three months.

♥ Active followers: you need followers who are engaged and responsive to your content. Encourage your followers to interact with you by asking them to double tap, comment, or tag a friend.

♥ Don't overuse hashtags: this can work against you on Instagram. Select carefully. Any more than three and you look thirsty. See page 239 for more information on Instagram from Instagram executive Claudine Cazian!

YOUNOW

Click the featured tab on the web or the search icon on the mobile app. There are four lists broken into categories.

♥ Top Broadcasters: shows broadcasters with highest number of likes within a broadcast.

♥ Editor's Choice: handpicked by YouNow staff for quality and topic accuracy. This is updated regularly.

♥ Top Fans: shows fans who have supported broadcasters with the highest value of gifts over the last twenty-four hours.

♥ Top Moment Creators: top moments on YouNow liked by users.

HOW NATHAN TRISKA DID IT

With just about four million followers, Nathan is at the top of social media ranks, but it wasn't a quick process. It took about two years of work.

Nathan started posting with 1,000 subs on YouTube and wasn't going anywhere fast. Then he started using YouNow, not even thinking of it as a platform—it just seemed like everyone was having fun on it. He started posting live and experimenting with the platform's hashtag system. "Some categories are really popular and hard to get noticed in. Others were a little easier. I started with #dance."

Success wasn't immediate, but he decided to keep at it, until he reached his tipping point. "A friend of mine encouraged me to jump on the much more populated #guys. The next day I got featured."

With five hundred views, that feature was a big moment. A tipping point isn't always three hundred thousand followers in twenty-four hours. Pushing from a few viewers to five hundred was like a gentle *tap* on a bee's nest, but it still got the bees buzzing!

The excitement and adrenaline from that new burst of action motivated Nathan to start taking his social media more seriously. He committed to going live every day for an hour. If he missed one day, he would make it up the next day and go on for two hours! He was on a roll. Within one year his audience grew and not just a little bit: he had hundreds of thousands of supporters, and it only kept growing.

TIPS FOR GOING LIVE FROM NATHAN TRISKA

1. Be yourself.
2. Collab—two personalities are better than one.
3. Focus on the people watching—not on yourself. Ask them what THEY want to see. If you don't care about your supporters, they won't be there forever.

WHAT TO DO WHEN YOU GET FEATURED AND/OR GO VIRAL

Congratulations! You've done it; you've had your tipping point and you're on the brains of people clicking around . . . for now. You may be the crème de la meme, but how do you maximize your window so you're not forgotten with yesterday's news?

As soon as you go viral, set up an email account that's strictly for business inquiries, and make sure you have it available in the bio of each of your platforms. Now is the time you're going to get hit up with offers, so make sure you read and respond to them! Some will be scams, some a waste of time, but it could also be Ellen or DigiTour reaching out! Sort through the real inquiries from the spam and think about how to leverage your moment into something more substantial. We'll talk about this more later on.

Selfie Made Mode:

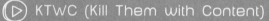 Your social media platform wants you to succeed! Utilize the tools they give you! Know how their features work!

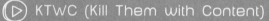 KTWC (Kill Them with Content)

Finding Your Platform

A PLATFORM IS
A JUMPING-OFF
POINT FOR YOU TO
GROW AND BUILD
YOUR AUDIENCE.

I can sit here and write out the pros and cons of each of these social platforms, but the truth is that until you get on and try them out for yourself, my words will be meaningless.

Below is the basic information for the top social platforms out there today. Most of them you probably already belong to. The ones that you don't? I recommend giving them a nice look over. At the very least make an account, and follow the top users. You might end up really liking a platform you never considered before.

> In August 2018, Musical.ly was re-branded and merged into TikTok. Everything can change at any time on social media. Some of the sites I mention may be different by the time you read this, but the advice is universally compatible.

FACEBOOK

Launched: February 2004

Founders: Mark Zuckerberg, Eduardo Saverin, Andrew McCollum, Dustin Moskovitz, and Chris Hughes

Number of users: 2 billion

Top five most followed accounts as of 2018:

1. Justin Bieber
2. Katy Perry
3. Michael Jackson
4. Vin Diesel
5. Rihanna

YOUTUBE

Launched: 2005

Founders: Chad Hurley, Steve Chen, and Jawed Karim

Number of users: 1.3 billion

Top five most subscribed channels as of 2018:

1. PewDiePie

2. T-Series

3. JustinBieber

4. HolaSoyGerman

5. Canal KondZilla

INSTAGRAM

Lauched: 2010

Founders: Kevin Systrom and Mike Krieger

Number of users: 700 million

Top five most followed accounts as of 2018:

1. Selena Gomez

2. Ariana Grande

3. Taylor Swift

4. Beyoncé

5. Kim Kardashian

YOUNOW

Launched: 2011

Founder: Adi Sideman

Number of users: 100 million

Top five most followed accounts as of 2018:

1. Tyler Brown

2. Wesley Tucker

3. Edwin Burgos

4. Timmy Connors

5. Zach Clayton

MUSICAL.LY

Launched: 2014

Founders: Alex Zhu and Luyu Yang

Number of users: 90 million

Top five most followed Musers as of 2018:

1. Jacob Sartorius

2. Baby Ariel

3. Loren Gray

4. Johnny Orlando

5. Kristen Hancher

SNAPCHAT

Launched: 2015

Founders: Evan Spiegel, Reggie Brown, and Bobby Murphy

Number of users: 191 million

Top five most followed accounts as of 2018:

1. kendalljenner

2. itsgigihadid

3. babybels777 (Bella Hadid)

4. khloekardashian

5. emrata (Emily Ratajkowski)

LIVE.ME

Launched: 2016

Founder: Fu Sheng (Cheetah mobile)

Number of users: 620 million

Top five most followed accounts as of 2018:

1. Roman Atwood

2. Markiplier

3. FouseyTube (Yousef Erakat)

4. JStuStudios

5. *The Dudesons*

VERIFY ME ALREADY!

How do you go from user to influencer on these platforms? And what's the benefit?

It helps if you're verified. But what does that mean?

Being verified means you have an authenticated account for a public figure, celebrity, or global brand. You would think that this process usually depends on the number of followers one has, but that's not the key factor to whether you'll get the blue check. Each platform has a different process to determine whether an account should be verified.

The benefit to being verified is you typically come up in searches first. Verified comments on posts usually receive preference and show up at the top. And verified accounts are more likely to be recommended to users to follow. And of course there's bragging rights.

Instagram currently doesn't allow you to submit and request a verification. If you know someone at the platform, you can submit manually through their process, which includes a team that evaluates the profile and determines if it's a brand, public figure, or celebrity. But unless you're a brand, public figure, or celebrity, you're going to be hard-pressed to make that connection.

Twitter briefly suspended their verification process as they worked some kinks out of it, but it's back up and running now. There's a form on their site, but make sure you can provide all the information they're asking you for, otherwise you're just wasting time (and time has value!).

YouTube has what they call their Partner Program to decide who gets verified: you should check them out and review their criteria.

Musical.ly calls it "getting a crown." Musical.ly determines who they give it to based on growth and engagement.

YouNow Partners require fan counts of five thousand or more, broadcast view minimum of one thousand per hour, consistent weekly broadcasts, and content that conforms to terms of service. You can apply on their site.

Snapchat verifies users via emoji icons. Verified users are called "Official Stories." Currently there is not a public submission form to verify your account and this is mostly reserved for celebrities like King Kylie (who left the platform while I was writing this book!). However, if you go to the contact page and attempt to connect with Snap staff through those means, you can make a case for why you should be verified. I caution you to take this step only if you believe you fit the criteria.

A Quick Word on Snapchat

"What about Snap, Meridith?" you may be saying to yourself right about now.

Here's the thing about Snap: there are no native-born Snap stars. You don't go to Snap to get discovered, unlike other platforms that can break you out. Snap is a good place to give more content to your audience once you have an audience.

Some people argue with me about this, but I know I'm right. Show me a Snap star and I'll show you where they were really born. It wasn't Snapchat. The purpose of this book is to help you find your way in social, and to build an audience, and for those purposes, Snap isn't where it's going to happen.

❌ ❌ ❌

#FIRST

Once you've scrolled through your preferred social platform twenty-plus times, you're sure to know what hashtags, conversations, drama, and memes are bubbling up by the hour. The trick to piggybacking your way into the social conversation is *being first*. If you see something going viral, it's the moment right before it explodes that matters. That's when you need to get clever and jump in: comment, react, or create your own version of the meme. One day it's a dancing hot dog gif, the next everyone is marking their location on Instagram as Singapore, Singapore. There was not a mass migration to Southeast Asia, but for some reason small, quirky, little things like that become the "inside joke" that everyone gets in on. Why? Why not? Social media is supposed to be fun after all, so have fun! OMG have the best time ever! WIG. Just don't be late to the party.

There is an incredible power to being first, hence the rush by many supporters to proudly type #FIRST on popular Instagram posts. If they're lucky enough to hit send in time, their comment and username will be prominently displayed. Having your username where millions of people will see it could capture attention. It may seem silly to you to race for #FIRST, but for those who are motivated by likes and follows, anything and everything is worth trying.

Your ability to go viral by being first has a direct correlation to you actually being first. Once a meme is all over your Twitter feed, it is too late to expect much social media growth from it. You need to jump on things that go viral and react, comment, repost, and be first.

Social media is a giant search engine. If something is blowing up, people are searching that hashtag to figure out why #howbouhdah is all over their timeline. If you can react/respond in the earliest moments, your contribution is boosted by searches and now you're in it. It's simple: the early bluebird (ahem, Twitter bird people) gets the worm.

This is not easy to do, but it is not by any means impossible. You need to be *obsessed* with your social media, constantly on top of what's going on. When you see a trend, tag, or challenge that looks like it's about to have a moment, *jump*, and do it fast. If the trend is already hot and you're late to the jump, that doesn't mean you can't participate. Just be realistic about your engagement expectations, and treat it like a practice run.

FIRST FANS

DigiTour was the first-ever social media tour. Putting our flag in the sand and reinforcing that accomplishment over time has made a big difference as far as our brand recognition, and our growth.

Similarly, the first bond an emerging talent makes with future fans is crucial. The attention you're able to give early on creates a foundation more akin to a friendship. That bond inspires and empowers the supporter to really go out and promote, even evangelize, on your behalf.

Early supporters will become your virtual and actual street team. These are the supporters who change their username to include yours. They repost your posts, they help spread the word, they'll defend you tirelessly against trolls, and they'll always show up first on the meet & greet at live events.

The upside for an early supporter is they tend to have more access to the creator. They get followed back. They get interaction. This is a big deal! That's why it's so important as a new creator to talk to early supporters and create bonds. This will be the foundation of your future fan base.

As the creator gets bigger, the early supporters feel a sense of ownership, which they should. A big reason the creator has grown to this point has to do with their help.

First supporters are raking in the benefits now more than ever since *guesting* became a thing. Guesting is when you have a viewer appear in their own video box beside you on a broadcast. Basically, stars can now feature their fans on their broadcast! This is currently available on Live.ly, YouNow, and Instagram Live. It's a great way to make supporters feel special. For supporters, part of the fun of following you is the chance of getting noticed. As a creator, make sure you take the time to do that. If your content is a one-way conversation of updates and selfies, you are sure to have followers tune out.

Massive stars cannot provide attention to every supporter. Maybe at one time they did, but as their following grows it's virtually impossible. You (yes, you reading this) can pick up where the big stars are lacking, and smartly jump in on comment threads on the various platforms of bigger creators. Could their fans be your future fans? Is their fav similar to you in some way? Same sense of humor or style? Is there something that connects you to that particular creator where you believe their audience would also be interested in your channels? Then go for it! Jump in and say hi.

A decade ago, the Jonas Brothers were performing in California, and there was a massive line of excited girls waiting outside their venue. A virtually unknown band at the time, Allstar Weekend (maybe you've heard of them?), was *also* outside the venue, realizing IRL that there was no good reason why these Jonas fans could not also be *their* future fans.

What did they do? They went up and down the line, acoustic guitars around their necks, and serenaded all the girls. They spoke to them, dare I say flirted as well, and left such an incredible impression. Shortly thereafter, Allstar co-headlined the very first DigiFest NYC.

You can do exactly what Allstar did—online—all day long. It's like an SAT question: Allstar is to the Jonas Brothers like (insert your name here) is to . . . ? Who are your Jonas Brothers? Can you pay attention to their fans and fill in where they may be slacking?

I've seen this tactic work so many times. Attention and interaction goes a long way, and if you can be active and interactive then you may be able to make some connections with your earliest supporters. These are the most important connections that you'll ever make.

It starts with jumping into the comments. If you don't have any yet, then jump in on someone who may appeal to your future fans and talk to the people in their thread—make connections!

THE POWER OF FANS, IN ACTION

As your circle of influence grows, you can find ways to respond and interact on a massive level. One social media superstar who has mastered fan engagement is Nash Grier. As he was building up his followers, he would do follow sprees

Me, Nash Grier, and Baby Ariel on the mainstage at PTTOW!

(where he would follow a bunch of his fans in one hour) and the incredibly smart #SelfieForNash, that led to thousands of his fans hashtagging their selfies thusly. I'm not sure Nash invented this concept, although I don't recall anyone doing it before him, but now #SelfieFor is a major hashtag tactic many talent use, notably Sebastian Olzanski.

These marketing gems created a flurry of posts, trending topics, and usually resulted in a few hundred thousand girls feeling like they were actually talking to/interacting with Nash.

I had the opportunity to work closely with Nash. He headlined several DigiFests in 2014 and 2015 and we even produced his South American tour in 2016. Nash held a brief tenure as the DigiTour creative director and as a part of his role, he would often accompany me to marketing events.

I'm a member of a group called PTTOW! This organization is comprised of two hundred and fifty CEOs and CMOs (chief marketing officers) from brands like Pepsi and Forever 21, and companies like iHeartRadio and Warner Bros. Records, and even celebs like Janelle Monáe, Charlie Puth, and Sarah Jessica Parker. I often was asked to talk about social media at their events. For one particular event in New York City, I invited Nash as my guest. I wanted him to help explain his influence to a bunch of people who were only just realizing what social media influencers are.

"That's a crazy room of people, if we do something we need to make it big," Nash said to me.

"Well, why don't we have a little fun with it? Let's show these people exactly what social media can do," I said.

Nash grinned and I knew I was in trouble.

We were scheduled to speak right after the event broke for lunch. The event itself was at Dream Hotel, and the lunch spot was a couple blocks away. Nash and I met the rest of the attendees at lunch, and planned to walk over with them.

When our food came out, Nash tweeted out to his audience that he was going to be heading to Dream Hotel in New York shortly.

"How many people do you think will show up?" I asked.

"Guess we'll have to go see." He smiled. No one else at the event knew what was about to happen!

Lunch ended, and the rest of the group, about four hundred people, began heading over to Dream Hotel. As we expected, as soon as we walked outside there was a noticeable buzz on the street. The closer we got to the hotel, the louder and more crowded it got.

All of the power execs were trying to figure out what was going on. "Who are they waiting for?" one of them asked me.

"I have no idea!" I lied.

Outside of the hotel was a wall of girls lined up on the sidewalk and spilling onto the street. The execs had their brows wrinkled, looking side to side. Nash and I exchanged a knowing smile and a quiet laugh; this was going to be fun.

The closer we got to the hotel door, the more I realized that we hadn't planned this out all the way. How was I, all five feet one of me, going to play security guard for Nash Grier? He's tall, like six-two, so it's not even like he just blends into a crowd. The girls recognized Nash, and a few of the execs realized the screams and shouts were indeed aimed at us. They were completely confused. Don't you love confusing adults?!

Nash said hello to some of the girls and we both ducked and ran inside the hotel. We needed to escape the crowd and set up our presentation, which meant the execs would have to fend for themselves!

I plugged Nash's phone into a big-screen projector, so all the execs could see what Nash was doing. They all made it into the room, laughing and amused by the spectacle.

"Who here is a social star? Please raise your hand," I said. No one responded. I guess no one had a following they wanted to brag about. "What do you think it feels like to have tens of thousands of notifications on your phone? Or to have millions of followers? Or to get hundreds of thousands of likes on everything you post?" As I said this, Nash's Twitter account was amassing a massive amount of likes and retweets on the big screen.

Nash stood up. "I want to show you guys what it's like. Let's take a group selfie." The group quickly did so, and Nash took the time to tag everyone in the room. He captioned the post: "Adults can have fun too."

"Alright, let's see how popular you are," I said with a wink. Within seconds, everyone was on their phones: "I just got thirty new followers!" said the exec from Coca-Cola. The numbers on Nash's screen just kept climbing and climbing. It was like watching a stock go crazy.

"So did you guys happen to notice some of our friends outside?"

"That was for you?" Someone gasped in disbelief in the second row.

"Well, for him," I said, gesturing toward Nash.

"Meridith wanted me to come and talk to you all about social media, but talking is boring. We wanted to show you how exciting it can be," Nash said.

"Should we bring someone up here?" I asked. "Find out why they like him so much?"

Everyone in the room nodded, warily. Seems like our session was a little outside of the box.

I sent an assistant down to the crowd outside with his FaceTime connected to Nash's phone on the screen. Once he was in the center of the excitement, he shouted to the group, "Does anyone want to FaceTime with Nash?" We could hear the screams through his FaceTime and something like a muted wailing from the street below us. My assistant turned the phone so we could FaceTime with the crowd.

Nash asked, "Does anyone want to come upstairs and hang out?"

Again, an overwhelming response from the crowd.

My assistant returned, flanked by two teary-eyed young girls who we invited to join us at the front of the room for a convo. But first, they embraced Nash like he was a long-lost friend, gripping him with white-knuckled intensity.

Once the hellos were said I settled them in and asked, "What made you come to the hotel today?"

"Because we love him."

"Do you consider him a celebrity?"

"We consider him a friend."

And right there was the learning moment: all the adults in the room who were out of touch with the connection social influencers have with their followers finally got it. It wasn't about being out of touch and on a pedestal. That was the old world. Nash was seen as a friend, not some unattainable presence on a screen. Even though these girls didn't have his phone number or hang with him on the weekends, they had a bond that made them feel connected, special, and valued as a part of his community.

Being an influencer is being the life of the party: organizing games, activities, conversation, keeping the energy up, and making everyone (even the quiet ones in the corner) feel special. It's a lot of work, but that's the only way you get the rewards.

Q&A with Simon Britton

Simon is really a totally normal guy who just happens to look like a Gap model.

His social media journey is a beyond-crazy success story and he's not in the uber-celeb category, either. Simon used YouNow because that's what all his friends were doing. He's friends with Nathan Triska, which definitely helped him grow, but his relatability is what made him Selfie Made. No fancy tricks, just putting in the work and using best practices. Simon's growing career is one that can serve as a model for how you can grow your audience, too.

How did you get started?

I started by going live on YouNow every day for fun and to make some friends online.

What was your tipping point/the moment you were featured or went viral or gained a burst of attention?

Two years ago around Christmastime on YouNow I started to do prank calls with some voice impressions and then a couple thousand people joined my broadcast and then they just continued to watch me and they all started to follow me on my other social medias.

Would you say there was a special bond with the first supporters?

Definitely; I share everything with my supporters and now that they have been around me for two or three years they know everything about me and I know a lot about them.

What advice can you give to aspiring creators to nurture that relationship with early supporters?

Get to know them; know them by their name and by their username. If you broadcast, ask your audience questions about themselves. Make it like a family.

How do you make so many people feel a one-to-one connection with you despite not being able to respond to each and every one?

Going live and interacting with everyone by reading comments, guesting, and asking questions makes it feel like a one-to-one connection—even if they are not getting their name called, at least they see that you are putting in effort to answer everyone and when they finally get their name called or question answered it makes it even more special.

What are your top tips that you would give to an aspiring creator?

You need to be consistent. You cannot just go a week without posting anything. If you don't keep supporters up to date with your life, they will lose interest in you. You have to give them a reason to keep following you.

How can you get an initial base when starting from nothing or almost no following?

Collaborate with people: this is the best way to grow in general, but especially when you are first starting out, to get that first boost. If you have no one to collaborate with, then post a lot across your social media platforms. The more you post, the more likely someone will come across your content.

How do you use different platforms differently?

♥ Musical.ly is just a fun social media platform where I can do funny, relatable skits or do some transition lip syncs that people will find cool.

♥ Twitter is for me to give my supporters updates on my life and also to talk about things people relate to.

♥ Insta is just to share pictures and goofy videos that they will enjoy.

♥ Snap is an hourly update on whatever I'm doing, also includes selfies and really random videos of my life.

♥ YouTube is for challenges and story times that I think people will find interesting and make them laugh.

♥ YouNow is to interact with my supporters and for them to get to know me and understand my personality more.

How important is touring and meeting fans to growing your audience?

Touring is very important because you finally get to meet supporters that may never be able to see you because they live in different states or countries. Also touring is like one big collaboration between content creators because you are bringing a bunch of creators' fan bases together at a show.

Can you give us a sample posting schedule that you might do in a day?

A typical day for me: one to three Musical.lys, one or two tweets, four to ten Snapchats; also I post one YouTube video a week and two to four Instagram pictures a week.

BE A BIG FISH IN A SMALL POND

With over four hundred hours of content being uploaded every minute on YouTube (according to YouTube CEO Susan Wojcicki), and approximately 65.7 years' worth of content, how can a new creator get noticed? Forget about ponds, this is more like an *ocean*.

If you're a new creator, what you have to offer is your time. Your time is currency, so think like an investor: where do you want to invest your time?

YouTube, with their lifetime of available content, may be a risky investment for new creators. Your content may be killer, but what are the real chances of a brand-new channel with very few followers popping up?

What new creators *don't* have is leverage. By leverage I mean that newbies are an unproven entity: why should YouTube feature your channel when there's a bunch of others who are already bringing in advertiser money?

A great way to build your brand and connect with future fans is to focus on smaller, newer social media platforms. In other words, get out of the ocean, and into a pond.

> What you have to offer is your time: what you need is leverage.

Now I wouldn't advise you to completely ignore the big guys. YouTube, Instagram, and Snap are important ways to nurture your base once you have one, and even when you don't you should be using those platforms to establish your voice and point of view. But to really find future fans, go where others are not. There is less distraction and more opportunity to stand out.

Cameron Dallas jumped on Vine before the masses. He also used Instagram to brand himself as a model. He leveraged the platforms and all they could offer him.

Baby Ariel dedicated time to Musical.ly before anyone else and they featured her to every new person who signed up, which resulted ultimately in her amassing twenty million followers.

Nathan Triska couldn't get noticed until he started going live on YouNow. Spending time on the smaller platforms where there's more one-on-one communication allowed these social media stars to get featured.

For me, starting DigiTour was a jump out of the big ocean of the music industry/record labels. I could have stayed in A&R at Columbia for the rest of my life, but what would have been the odds of me running the company and being my own boss? I didn't want to use my brain to further someone else's business; I wanted to use it for myself!

> ## If you want to move up, you have to move out.

New platforms *need* talent. That need gives you leverage. The early talent will get rewarded.

However, for every Musical.ly there's a platform that didn't work. If you've invested time into one of these, then your investment did not pay off. So before you commit to a new platform, think: could it become the next YouTube? If so, invest your time, let the community managers get to know you, and watch the love you get in return. If they feature you prominently, you can be growing your fan base in your sleep.

Reaching a community manager sounds harder than it actually is. There's always a contact email available on your platform's website, or you can get really crafty and Google "community manager," the platform name, and "LinkedIn." Just be warned: you only get one chance at a first impression. Community managers do not owe you anything and if they don't respond to you, it is not a personal slight, it's just the way it works. If you want to connect with them, introduce yourself and start a meaningful relationship: be polite, and create a short and simple intro. Three-page emails will not get read.

A big app can't hold your hand and shower you with attention and love. Not because they don't want to, they just don't have the resources. Once you have the love on a smaller platform, you can drive your base over to the big platforms and then they will notice you and your following, too.

Selfie Made Mode:

▷ There are perks to being first.
▷ Be a big fish in a small pond.
▷ If time is a currency, where are you spending it?

Collabing = Networking

COLLABING: CREATING CONTENT WITH PEOPLE WHO HAVE A LARGER AND/OR DIFFERENT FOLLOWING THAN YOURS, IN AN EFFORT TO CROSS-PROMOTE AND HELP DRIVE EYEBALLS AND NEW FOLLOWERS.

Me as one of the Lollipop Guild in
The Wizard of Oz

When I was ten I decided I wanted to be an actor and sought to elevate my opportunities in small-town suburbia into something a little more major. Initially I tried out for our community theater production of *The Wizard of Oz*, and while I was sure I'd be cast as Dorothy, I settled for one of the Lollipop Guild munchkins. It was typecasting. Playing a small male munchkin with a sideways expression (I was a purist) was not my ideal summer plan, but it was me paying my dues to get to know Ms. Wallach, the theater director, a little bit better.

Important to the art of networking is knowing the right time to ask for something. There is a dance, a give-and-take, and if you come right out and shamelessly ask for what you want, it's probably not going to get you far. So there I was, after my final performance, still dressed as a member of the

Lollipop Guild, and I marched up to Ms. Wallach and said, "So what's next for me and this whole acting thing?"

What I really wanted to know was if she had any agents who might take a meeting with me.

Ms. Wallach laughed. "Meridith, you're ten. Why don't you try and relax." This was a reaction I elicited in my networking pursuits most of my life. "But I do know one person you could talk to."

The internet has transformed the *art* of networking into a game of quantity: likes, follows, and comments. It's not cool to just connect with your friends anymore. Strangers are fair game and everyone is a lifestyle brand. The cream rises to the top and the people/accounts/channels that rise to great heights carry a newfound responsibility to have a message and a point of view.

As a member of Generation Z, you are the first generation to spend your entire life with the answer to almost every question at your fingertips. When I first sought out an agent at ten and later an internship at fifteen, I was an internet-less girl with a major hunger to get out and make things happen. I remember the primitive form of googling: it was literally asking people questions IRL. How retro.

I wonder what I would have done if I were ten years old post–internet domination. I probably would have sent friend requests to every agent on social, which probably could have turned out pretty weird. The internet gives you everything at your fingertips, but there's not a great way to screen what's real and what's fake. There are a lot of catfishers and rabbit holes.

My advice is to employ a little bit of the old school mixed with the internet. Ask people you know for recommendations, triple-check someone or something you come across to make sure it's legit, and remember that just friending someone doesn't make you friends or truly connected.

If you want to work with someone or form a real relationship in building your online brand, reaching out and writing a personal note goes a long way.

Networking in today's world requires sifting through more volume, but if you have a sense of what you want, you can better figure out who you need to connect with. Perhaps a community manager at a social platform, or a partnerships lead at a multichannel network. Maybe even someone at your favorite brand you can strike up a relationship with around a future deal. I've signed up people to perform at DigiTour who reached out directly to me. It doesn't happen all the time, but when it's handled respectfully, and they have what I'm looking for, it can and does happen.

Or, maybe it's other talent you want to connect with, for collabs. The point is, all these things are within reach (or all within a tweet)!

One of the reasons Selfie Made as a concept exists is because of the world of opportunity that the internet gives to everyone. Not just the person who has connections or lives near a major city, but literally anyone who has a vision and work ethic. It's all at your fingertips.

And so Ms. Wallach connected me to an agent. He sent me on many auditions, including Madison Square Garden's *A Christmas Carol*—let's just say I didn't get the part, but my little brother left as Tiny Tim. Back to the drawing board!

HOW MUCH IS A SHOUT-OUT WORTH?

I heard a rumor that JJ Hannon actually took his expensive Yeezys off his feet and gave them to Hunter Rowland in exchange for a shout-out. This . . . would not surprise me. I know plenty of people who would happily part with their favorite accessory for a shot at getting closer to their dreams of social stardom. The hustle some up-and-comers have makes all the difference in their path toward a following.

Being aligned with larger influencers can create a halo effect. We saw this clearly with the many people who kept Cameron Dallas company over

Me, Chad "Dad" Grier, former Digi staffer Amanda Bodenstein, and cofounder of Bonnaroo Rich Goodstone at Bonnaroo 2015

the years. From his once assistant/manager that he helped promote into a full-blown social star, to his personal photographer and friend Bryant Eslava, who now boasts millions of his own dedicated followers.

At DigiFest Toronto one year, I was walking with Nash Grier's dad, Chad, who at the time was managing both his son and Cameron Dallas. The festival had thousands of attendees and over fifty stars (Nash, Cameron, Fifth Harmony, Caspar Lee, PointlessBlog, Connor Franta, Trevor Moran, Kian & Jc, and Sam Pottorff, to name a few).

Chad was extremely hands-on with his son's merch business (rightfully so, as we'll discuss later), and asked me if I could show him where it was set up so he could count the T-shirts for the boys.

"No problem," I said.

And no problem did I think it would be. I escorted my new friend, who stood almost a foot and a half taller than me, toward the merch booth. As we talked and walked, we were enveloped by teen girls. Not ten or twenty, but hundreds.

I scanned the grounds. Was there a lost star wandering out from the meet & greet room? Why were the girls shrieking and closing in on *me*? And then I heard it: "DAD! DAD! Can we take a selfie?"

They were all freaking out over Nash's dad! Here at DigiFest he wasn't just a football coach from the South with three sons, he was a famous dad with a larger social following than some of the talent we booked at our events.

Influencers inevitably share pictures of the people close to them, who then also become known and adored. They also represent a direct line to the people some fans love the most.

My favorite halo effects are always the beloved pets of my favorite social stars. Matthew Espinosa's dog, Burnie, now boasts almost 200,00 followers on Instagram, and has his own business email. How many followers do you think Jacob Sartorius' pillow would have?

The thing to keep in mind here is that social media stars are people, just like you and me. They have family and friends they care about, and a lot of them work very hard to also engage with their fans. But it is not their responsibility to make you famous! It is yours and yours alone.

Max & Harvey

Q&A with Max & Harvey

Max and Harvey are fifteen-year-old twin brothers from the United Kingdom who are singers and Musical.ly stars. They have boy-band looks *and* boy-band charm. They are polite and quirky and of course their English accents set them apart from their American competition. They rose quickly in social media rankings, using mostly Musical.ly to boost their popularity in the UK, which quickly moved across the pond and gave them a presence in the United States. Max and Harvey have a book out, a BBC show in the UK, and are about to sign a record deal.

How did you guys get started?

Max: When we were younger we used to always sing and be a part of shows in different theaters in London's West End. By the time we were thirteen we took our singing to social media and people really liked our videos, so we kept going and it built from there.

What was your tipping point?

Max: It was when we first got featured on Musical.ly—we did a short cover of "Love Yourself" by Justin Bieber and it really connected with people.

What's your best advice for someone who's just starting out with no following who wants to grow?

Harvey: My piece of advice to people who want to grow their

following is to find something they're really good at and just show it to the world. No matter what people say, or if people make fun of you, you have to carry on because eventually you'll get there. Everyone can

Tim Bryne, Mike Daly, Ken Bunt, Max & Harvey, me, Chris, Cassie Petrey, and Mio Vukovic at the signing of Max & Harvey to RMI/Disney Records, 2018 (Disney photo by Lester Cohen)

do whatever they put their mind to; they just have to persevere and keep going.

When did you realize you had fans/supporters for the first time?

Max: It was when we got noticed for the first time just walking down the street. We were so surprised that it was happening to us!

Once you have an initial base, what are the most important tips one can do to keep that audience engaged?

Max: DON'T EVER STOP! Your fans on social media follow you because they enjoy the different content you post, and if it's not there, they can easily go find someone else to follow.

Do you think live broadcasting is important?

Harvey: I think that live broadcasting is a good aspect of social media because it really shines a light on your personality and it helps your fans really understand who you are! It's an especially great way to interact with fans who live far away and may not get as many opportunities to come to shows.

How important is meeting your fans IRL?

Harvey: There's nothing better than meeting our fans in real life. It's all good when you can see people's screen names and comments, but when you can match a name to a face it's awesome. We love performing for them and it's genuinely one of my and Max's favorite things to do.

When posting covers do you aim to select specific songs?

Max: We tend to choose songs that we know well and that we know our fans will like. We don't always go for the newest songs like a lot of other people and instead go for something everyone already knows and loves.

I notice you have a very funny style of captioning on Instagram. Did you always do it this way? How did you develop your voice on social?

Harvey: When I caption on Instagram it's basically just my style of humor. We've done this for a while now, the main reason being we want to give our fans more than just a two-word caption. It helps them understand us more and people seem to like it. In all honesty, when I write those captions, I genuinely think of it as I'm typing, as you can probably tell. . . .

You're really musicians first, using social media to help gain exposure. How do you approach social media differently than someone seeking just social media fame?

Max: We work really hard to make everything on our own and I think that helps us stand out. We one day hope to be proper artists performing in large venues, and social media is a great way for us to build our fan base and help us get there.

Do you have advice for an aspiring musician who wants to grow in a similar way?

Max: Always put your music first if it's what you've always wanted to do! This will help people understand that you are a musician first. Once you've established this you can use social media to build up your fan base and experience until you think you're ready to start touring and growing more as a musician.

Do you mind if you're called a "social media star," or do you try to avoid that label as you pursue your music?

Max: We don't mind at the moment because it's what we are, but when we get older we'd hope to have the title of "artists."

How do you use other platforms to drive back to your cover or song post?

Harvey: We usually just post a cover on one platform so that it gets more engagement in that one place instead of it being spread around on others. If we post an original song on YouTube, we'll use the other platforms to post short clips of the song so that, hopefully, people will go over to YouTube to watch the full thing.

What platform has been the most important one for your growth?

Harvey: The platform that mainly started it all for us was Musical.ly! Now we're working on transferring that following to our other platforms as well as expanding our age range all around to be able to appeal to all ages from seven to eighteen and sometimes even lower or higher!

CHASE KEITH PUTS THE WORK IN

To get a full sense of every stage of social media stardom, I wanted to talk to a few young, emerging social talents who are not quite at the Loren Gray or even Tyler Brown level of thirty million or five million followers, respectively, but that are under one million. Talking to people at different stages of growth is helpful to really understand the various components at each point that help elevate your content and keep you going.

One who caught my attention was Chase Keith. Chase was on my radar initially because he DM'ed me on Instagram. He was interested in being a guest at one of our Digi dates. His message was polite and he was clearly hungry to grow. Side note: I read all my DMs!

With five hundred thousand followers, Chase's career is coming along nicely, but it was not long ago he was inching along with tens of thousands. I gave him a call and asked him a bunch of questions to understand what helped him go from a few thousand to a few hundred thousand.

It all began, as it did for most of the rising social media stars of the last twenty-four months, with Musical.ly. However, for Chase it wasn't an immediate goal to become a Muser or even a social media star for that matter. He downloaded the app as a joke. A few of his friends did the same thing. But after making comedy vids using the top hashtags, his videos started getting noticed and he wasn't thinking of it as a joke anymore. When he accumulated five thousand followers, he was reached out to by Kaylee Halko, a much bigger Muser, who has five million followers. The two did a duet. Post-collab, Chase experienced a boost of a few hundred new followers.

While it was a modest boost, it served to motivate Chase to keep going. By continuing to post and using trending tags, he accumulated fifty thousand!

Chase set his sights on getting featured. If he could get a feature, he thought it would get him closer to a crown, which would get him closer to the big following he desired. Chase took it step-by-step. He reached his goal and got featured, which was excellent. But then he needed a new goal: to get featured three times. He was able to achieve this in a short window of time.

The feature process on Musical.ly has changed a bit, but when Chase was featured only twenty to forty vids were featured per day, and if you scored one of the spots you'd get a couple hundred thousand likes. Soon after his features, a Chase Keith Instagram fan page popped up: a big moment for Chase.

I wanted to better understand why his videos were getting featured and if he knew what separated them from the content he'd posted previously, so I texted Chase and asked him as much. He answered right away: "I was doing something different than everyone else. People were getting featured for lip sync, gymnastics, etc. . . . I was doing edited comedy routines."

"Any other tips on creating content?"

"Be aware of how your content is being reacted to!"

The features helped Chase double his followers, and soon he was beginning to collab with other creators. His next goal was a crown. He ended each Musical.ly with saying "CROWN CHASE" and his supporters also would post and tag that to get the app's attention. At a hundred thousand followers, Chase crossed his next goal off his list: he got his crown! With each little victory (or big victory) he saw his base grow and realized he was in Selfie Made mode, proactively inching toward his ultimate goal of being a social media star.

The hustle is real, and the hard work is real. Chase comes home from school and posts. He works on posting, thinking of ideas, does homework, goes to bed, and the cycle repeats. He reinvests his money from going live and doing app promos into hiring photographers to shoot better photos on Instagram. Since doing this, his likes per photo went from an average of three- to four thousand to eight- to ten thousand. He tells me he works hard every day and rarely takes breaks.

Chase Keith's Rules for Social Media Growth

▷ Reinvest to make your content better. Get a ring light or a small setup to make better content for your supporters.

▷ Research trending tags.

▷ Tell your supporters via Snap or Insta Live when you're posting a new Musical.ly or Insta photo so that you get maximum engagement right away. I'll say, "Hey, I'm uploading at 3 P.M. and will be replying to comments." This gets the engagement up. I encourage supporters by offering DMs to fans who like and comment.

▷ Use captions that encourage engagement on Instagram. For example, "tag a friend who needs a smile today."

▷ Tag brands you're wearing. This can help get you noticed on a popular brand tag.

• • •

THE NETWORKING MAGICIAN

One of the best networkers I know is Collins Key.

Collins is someone you probably know, but when I met him he was just a teen magician with big aspirations. He was traditionally talented, he had charisma, he could work a crowd, he understood timing, and he was polite and professional. I'm not saying you don't see those things in the internet world, but let's just say they're not always as common.

There was one issue standing in the way of Collins making it big: he had no audience. He had occasional gigs at the Hollywood members-only magician club Magic Castle, which was great for his magician skills, but super-exclusive clubs don't usually help you develop a fan base. Most of the audiences there are magic-loving adults dressed in (strictly required) suits and ties. Not exactly Collins' future fans.

I met Collins through mutual friends who worked for his dad's wedding entertainment company. Chris and I were invited to see him do magic one night at the Magic Castle, which looks like a *Harry Potter* set right in the middle of the Hollywood Hills. We had a great time at the show, and immediately after his performance, Collins (and his dad) came by our table and started to pick our brains. By the end of the night, I had agreed to work with Collins as a social media consultant.

I wanted to help Collins because I thought he had a lot of potential to make it big. He was teed up to be on the new season of *America's Got Talent* and was planning to go all the way. This had all the makings of a tipping point, but as you now know, that's just the beginning.

"You have to spend some time getting your socials up. Let's set a schedule, let's get rolling!" I told him.

"I'm going to be on TV, that's how I'll get my name out there. What do I need social media for?" He wasn't being difficult; he was focused on his work. And I don't mind that at all!

"Trust me," I said. "When you're on *AGT*, every teen watching is going to be looking you up and following you. If they see you don't take their world seriously, they won't bother following. You may never get another chance to engage this quantity of people."

I saw it click in Collins' head. "Okay, I trust you," he said.

During each victorious week of *AGT*, Chris and I crafted Collins' social strategy and live tweeted from his account. I invited friends of mine who were social stars like thatsojack and jennxpenn to sit in the audience of *AGT* in exchange for a shout-out on social. This was a win-win collab for them and for Collins. These social stars had a fun night out, and Collins got acknowledgment from social stars with devoted fan bases.

As he progressed toward the finals, we had Collins Key trending worldwide on Twitter. He went from just a few hundred friends to an audience of tens of thousands of extremely active fans.

The winter of that year, we produced DigiFest LA for four thousand fans at the Hollywood Palladium. Collins was there, hanging with us backstage, and he asked me to introduce him to the various talent, from Troye Sivan to Connor Franta and Kian Lawley to Hoodie Allen and Noah Cyrus. Even Bella Thorne and viral fav Rebecca Black were backstage hanging out, as well as Justin Bieber's . . . security team. They arrived three hours early to prep for Bieb's arrival, an arrival which never happened. So there's that.

"I'll introduce you, Collins, but don't get your hopes up. These are pros, and you can't just ask them to collab with you. It might get awkward."

"You trust me this time, Meridith."

Most of the DigiTour talent would never have done a traditional collab with Collins because the unwritten rule of collabing is each party wants to get something in return. Usually you see talent of similar-sized audiences cocreating content and tagging each other to grow their audiences respectively. Many of the top-ranked talent are extremely wary of people trying to use them for their numbers. And Collins, even though he'd been on *AGT*, and was an emerging talent with tens of thousands of followers, would stand zero chance next to these heavyweights.

I introduced Collins to the talent. They were friendly, but slightly cautious. But Collins was true to his word. To each person I introduced him to, he said, "Hi, I'm Collins Key, can I show you a close-up magic trick?"

Eight out of ten people said sure.

Then he asked if he could film it. Five out of ten said sure.

He ended up with five vids for his channel, with some of the biggest social talent on YouTube. They didn't copromote the content, but Collins was still able to push it out, tag their names, and catch the attention of people who followed his video's costars.

As more people got to know Collins and his numbers grew, he set up actual collabs. He also opened on tour for Demi Lovato. I reached out to some more of Digi's big social friends and offered them tickets to see Demi in concert in exchange for shout-outs for Collin. Who doesn't want tickets to see Demi?

Just like I did with my theater teacher when I was ten, Collins employed smart networking and collabing. If you have something to offer, a great idea, a space to shoot, an awesome camera or equipment, access to an awesome event (tickets to Digi!?), then use that . . . that's Networking 101.

Now, Collins Key is COLLINS KEY. He doesn't need me to introduce him backstage, and he doesn't have to sneak vids and offer tickets to get people to provide shout-outs. He's the one turning down collab offers; he's the one with millions of followers and more opportunities than he can actually fulfill.

The moral of the story: you need to be creative and realistic. A huge social star is not going to help you launch your career just because you're a super-nice person. They appreciate your support as a fan and will take pics in the meet & greet line, or maybe reply to one of your tweets or comments on Insta, but they don't owe you a collab.

Still, collabing is one of the best ways to succeed in social media.

Selfie Made Mode:

▷ For collabs, start small. Find someone on your same playing field; they may have some followers that are not following you.

▷ Go to events: DigiTour, VidCon, Playlist Live, and pull a Collins Key! Get as much content with the big guys as possible to post and tag later.

▷ Think who your future audience is: is it the same people following Loren Gray? Baby Ariel? Or Dude Perfect? Fish where the fish are, but first know what kind of fish you're looking for. Then dive in and start talking to fans posting on those channels/pages. Engage in convo and be social.

7

The Art
of Cross-
Platforming

PROTECT YOUR INTERNET-ITY

1. Select a username on ALL platforms (even the ones you may not start using right away).
2. Find a brandable spot to film and film there for the bulk of your content.
3. Set up a realistic schedule.
4. Get in the conversation: use trending tags, jump in on challenges, and try to be early.

Your identity on the internet, or your internet-ity if you will, is something you want to build on and promote. However if you have JohnSmithRocks on Twitter and JohnSmith_101 on Instagram and JohnSmithIsCool on YouTube and YouNow . . . you're making it very difficult for people who may like you on one platform to find you on another (John Smith really needs a class on creativity, apparently).

When DigiTour produced Jack & Jack's headline tour in 2014, Jack Johnson received a cease and desist letter from folk-pop singer Jack Johnson. Not because he was imitating him blatantly but because his Twitter handle was so popular, folk-pop Jack Johnson thought social-media Jack Johnson was confusing his audience.

Social-media Jack Johnson knew his followers didn't think he was pop-rock Jack Johnson. But these are the predicaments you find yourself in when vying for social handles in a world where many people have the same name.

I can't begin to tell you the number of talents I've worked with who have regretted their early YouTube usernames. Andrea Russett was once known on YouTube as GETTOxFABxFOREVER. Ricky Dillon was PICKLEandBANANA. While they both opted for something less abstract as they matured in their internet careers, others have taken their brand and transformed it into something bigger.

If you're just starting out, it might make sense to ask yourself if there is a version of your name or a clever moniker based on the type of content you'll be posting, or even a character you want to play (ahem Miranda Sings) that could help create a memorable name that you can own across all of the big platforms. What is the brand you're building? Would someone wear it on a T-shirt or, thinking even bigger, could someone dress up like you for Halloween?

Not everyone is going to play a character like Miranda Sings, but the Halloween question helps you think about how well branded you are or want to be. If someone was tasked with re-creating your brand—literally for Halloween, or less literally, for a license to create merchandise, etc.—would they be able to do it?

Google is a search engine, and in building a brand and leveraging your social you want someone to type in one thing and have everything come up. Don't send your future fans on a scavenger hunt unless you're doing it on purpose because you're cross-platforming!

You may decide it's Musical.ly that most speaks to your style of content creation or personality. Or perhaps live broadcasting is your thing. What you'll eventually discover (and you will discover now if you listen to me) is that while one platform may become your main creative outlet, you can't ignore the rest. Cross-platforming is *essential* to growing your social profile. In case that term is new to you, here's the bottom line: you need to find a way to tell your whole story across the various social platforms.

While almost no successful social influencers exclusively post on one platform, many do select one as their main platform where they spend the most time, post the most, and develop their online personality. The other platforms then become a way to promote the main one. Rather than floundering across several platforms, focus your time and energy on the one that's right for you, but have a plan for all the others, too.

To be clear, you can't just repost what you published on one platform across the others. That's a no-no. The last thing I want as a consumer of internet content is to see you put the same thing in the same way on different platforms. That will definitely have me tune out. Seriously, why don't you just hold on while I go take a nap? You need to be creative and weave your posts together and tell a little something different with each one. Each platform has a certain style and specialty, so your content for each platform should be created accordingly.

By posting across platforms, cross-promoting your content and yourself across all channels, you are maximizing the exposure of what you're posting and widening the net of who will see it and how they'll consume it.

No matter how much redundancy you have in your audience (fans subscribing to more than one platform, thus when you add up your whole following you count a few people twice or even three or four times!), there are bound to be a few people on each platform that prefer *that* platform.

My personal favorite platform is Instagram. If there's something posted on Facebook or Twitter, I might miss it, but if someone I follow on Insta posts something, chances are I saw it. If someone I like isn't keeping up with their Insta, then I'm not engaging with them. Without finding a way to connect the narrative you're telling platform to platform, you may miss key engagement.

Evan Britton

Founder of FamousBirthdays.com Tells You How To Have A Famous Birthday!

FamousBirthdays.com has become a goal for many aspiring creators, similar to the coveted blue check mark, Musical.ly crown, or touring slot on DigiTour. The oh-so-cool, brag-worthy shoutout on social from the FamousBirthdays on YOUR birthday is a major milestone for any influencer's career. Through FamousBirthdays, Evan has celebrated with over one hundred thousand social media influencers. You want to be next?

How did you start FamousBirthdays?

We started as a website focused on traditional celebs—to learn more about them. We saw more interest and demand in social media stars and it was an underserved market on the web. I didn't have the idea to build the celebrity platform for this next generation's stars, it was the users that showed us the demand.

What's your traffic like?

We have eighteen million unique users per month.

How can you get a Famous Birthday?

It's a combination of a few factors:

♥ User interest

♥ What's happening with a celebrity—in terms of engagement, or their projects.

A lot of it's driven by our user demand —that's a sign to us that people have real fans. We're looking for people our fans care about.

What's your advice to aspiring social media creators?

There are so many people building followings. Don't get discouraged if it's not happening yet.

In terms of how to really grow, engagement is important. People talk about followers, but that doesn't matter as much as engagement, by which I mean real people that care. Not inflated engagement, real engagement.

The other thing I think is a niche. It's important to have a niche because there are so many creators. Go after some specific thing. That's a way to a larger fan base.

A lot of new stars on a new platform. That's a platform niche. On a bigger platform you want to have a speciality within that, that way people can really know you.

Another thing is to really care about your fans. The big stars talk about how they grew. They talk about how they responded to every comment they got. Some people talk about how social stars have luck but I always fight that. I don't think it's luck, I think it's talent and hard work. It's a lot of work. To manually respond to every comment takes time but you're gonna build strong connections with less people. Look at Rihanna or Beyoncé's Instagram accounts, they have one hundred million followers. The social stars may have one to five million, but their engagement percentage is higher.

Any final thoughts?

Be really good at one platform, then okay at five. There's only so much time, and you want those deep connections. And tweet us and say hi!

GAMIFICATION

Think of cross-platforming as a scavenger hunt. Make sure to find a hook for people to come back for more, and don't forget: with every great game comes a prize or a way to win.

For some creators that is literal. Take Nate Garner, for example. His way of exciting fans is through an almost constant stream of giveaways and contests: from a new iPhone, to flying with him on a private jet. He's like the Publishers Clearing House of social channels! Prizes aren't usually so extensive: a follow, a DM, a comment back, or even just a like. These *digital autographs*, as I call them, carry mega weight and mean the supporter is getting noticed, appreciated, and that makes all the work of being a good fan so worth it! To a lot of fans, they'd rather have that personal connection with their fav than a free iPhone!

I'm sure you have seen other supporters note these precious moments in their Twitter or Insta bios: "on this date this person followed!" It is a badge of honor.

Selfie Made Mode:
The Content Creator Checklist

- ▶ Get on a schedule
- ▶ Upgrade your setup
- ▶ Get pro images
- ▶ Get pro design for your account headers
- ▶ Set up a business email
- ▶ Create initial merch
- ▶ Keep it up!

Finding Your Voice/ Building Your Brand

Whether you call yourself (or strive to call yourself) a creator, an influencer, social media star, or internet boss, what you are or what you're working to become is a *lifestyle brand*.

What does that mean? In today's internet world, every Instagram account or YouTube channel is a hub for content. But, more than just a place to watch a video, these channels have become living communities. There is power in this, power that influencers have been able to harness.

A community comes with a set of cultural values, ideas, and characteristics. And while some channels, you may argue, are not *that* deep, I could argue back that each successful channel with a real following *does* have a community with those components.

Pre-internet, there were fewer choices in the mainstream as far as lifestyle brands. Most of them, just like the radio stars and TV stars of the past, were not created independently but were products of major corporations who *manufactured* an image and brand. Then the media would help to reinforce these brands as the defining pop culture of the corresponding generation.

Gen Z threw this whole concept in the garbage. A handful of communities or brands did not have the power to represent Gen Z. It is a generation too complex, diverse, and clued in to the world around it for it to be dictated by the mass media. Youth culture wasn't always so sophisticated, so it was easier to generate it in a boardroom. Not anymore.

That's the beauty of today's lifestyle brands: they are crafted by creators, individuals with a POV, and they are usually #nofilter and honest. They are not manufactured, overproduced, or contrived. Therein lies the power: influencers are trusted voices because they are driven by raw interest and passion.

(Usually.)

The lifestyle brands of this generation are innumerable, so there are no hard-and-fast rules. Some communities on the internet cater to tens of millions and some to tens. That's because some fans want to engage with a large community, and some with only a few.

When you find social media success, you will have an audience who follows what you post and even looks forward to it the same way others may DVR their favorite shows on TV. What you become known for will dictate what your brand is. That means if a picture of you holding a cat goes viral, your brand is now about cats. Even if you hate cats. Even if that's the first time you ever held a cat, and your grandmother had to bribe you to hold it. You and that cat will forever be linked.

Your brand will begin with your content but, if you play your cards right, it can evolve into many lucrative extensions. If your brand is cats, there are plenty of companies and products geared toward cat lovers that could make great brand partners for you. There are worse ways to make money than as the face of cat toys!

You want a more exciting example? Take Jojo Siwa. Jojo has music, a book, a TV special on Nickelodeon, and a hard-to-miss line of hair bows sold in Walmart, Target, and T.J. Maxx (and more) that are as big as her personality. She found a way to visually brand herself (the bright-colored outfits and bows the size of Texas), she honed a voice (outgoing, confident, and positive), and she's successfully found ways to continue to pump out content while layering in other revenue streams for her brand. Jojo represents *something*, and her Siwanators follow her because they like what that is.

Tyler Oakley has become well known for his alignment and advocacy for the LGBTQ community. He stands for something and is vocal about his point of view. He uses his platform as a place to not only share his pop culture commentary, but also to amplify important messages he believes in. As a result, he's a magnet for like-minded people. Tyler creates community and culture: the core of a good lifestyle brand.

I always ask talent I'm working with:

> WHY would someone who doesn't know you personally care to read your posts, look at your photos, or watch your vids? What's unique? What's relatable? And what's shareable about what you're going to do?

If you can't answer that question right away, don't worry! If you *can* answer that question, be aware that your answer may evolve. Once you start posting you might realize people love your style, or the way you caption, or maybe they find you funny and relatable, or maybe you have content that resonates with a large group. (For example, meet & greet poses! Slime! Great DIY room décor!)

The trick is to be yourself and then supercharge it. Maybe your strong values and political POV resonate with a group. Maybe you love reading and can talk about books. Almost every social media star I work with says one thing that's the same: "I'm just myself."

If you can't quite figure out what makes you unique, here's an exercise for you: write about yourself. Not a couple sentences, but it doesn't have to be a book, either. In the back of this book there's space for you to write down who you are, your basic biographical information (family members, pets, where you go to school, etc.), and then write down what you love. Video games? Movies? It doesn't matter what it is; if you can get down a few paragraphs' worth of information about yourself, you may find some recurring themes about who you are and what makes you stand out.

Still stumped? Hey, it's not always easy to figure yourself out, so don't beat yourself up about it. I'll teach you the oldest trick in the book: just pick something. If you're not sure what you like, just pick something and do it. I don't care what it is. Join a knitting group. Start jogging. Get a piece of soap and cut pieces off it and film it (who knew this would become a thing?). Learn every single line from your favorite movie. It doesn't really matter what you do, just do something. And take some pics while you're at it and include all your friends on social in your adventure!

If you randomly pick something to do and you like it, great! If you don't like it, no big deal; you now have more information from which to work from. Don't overthink it; just keep it moving.

Instead, like always, just truth bomb it. "Hey (name of your friend), I'm working on my social media and trying to figure out what my brand is. What do you think?" If your friends are social literate, they'll know exactly what you mean. If they're not, you may have to explain the word *brand*, but by now you should be an expert on that, and they're lucky they've met you and your wise brain.

You may be surprised at how others see you, or you may have your own opinion of yourself validated. Either way, remember that everyone has an opinion, and those opinions are usually biased on the way they see the world. You don't have to believe everything everyone says about you, but remember: what you're doing here is trying to figure out how you'll come across to people you don't know on social media. You're not asking your friends to tell you who you are, you're asking them to tell you how they *perceive* you. No matter what, no one knows you better than you know you.

I didn't really realize what I wanted to do or what my brand was until my first ever DigiFest NYC. It was completely sold out and packed wall-to-wall with teen girls. That's when I realized who my target fan base was, and it changed my business forever.

Finding your supporters and understanding why they're drawn to your content (in my case our live tours and experiences) helps you fine-tune and make it even better. As long as you have an eye on how people are responding and you're actively trying to improve, you'll grow.

✦ ✦

DON'T TAKE YOURSELF TOO SERIOUSLY!

It's hard sometimes to laugh at yourself. Or purposefully post that pic that shows your acne breakout or your chin rolls. But we all love a derp face! Being relatable is one of the most important aspects to connecting with an audience. I'm not saying you can't take a posed pic with great lighting (we all should be a little extra sometimes!), but you should also have #nofilter moments, to remind everyone that you're just a regular person.

My ride for the day, DigiFest 2015

Before you can find where you belong online (aka your tribe), you need to put yourself out there. And before you do *that*, you need to have the confidence to take the first step. Confidence is a funny thing. IRL or online, when you're a teenager, confidence is probably the most challenging thing to possess. When I was in high school I was hyperfocused, almost so ambitious it was funny, and when my big ideas or plans rubbed my peers the wrong way I would freeze and get super-defensive. I didn't understand at fifteen why my friends didn't think getting an internship was cool or why they'd whisper behind my back when I'd describe my future career plans. In hindsight

Me and Chris getting ready for DigiFest Houston

it was all too much. I was a little ahead of my time and my ambition was mistaken for gross narcissism. I didn't let it prevent me from being social, at least not up until one point . . .

IRL TROLLS

Me and former Digi team member Amanda Bodenstein ready for DigiFest Toronto!

Coming of age before the internet made things more black-and-white. If you didn't connect with your peers, then you had no friends. If there was nothing going on in your hometown, then you were probably bored.

Most of the influencers I work with at DigiTour are introverted outsiders with little skill for real-life socializing. Many of them were (and are) bullied in their own schools, sometimes to the point of resorting to homeschooling. High school requires conforming to the status quo, minimizing what makes you unique, and blending into the crowd. But with social media, you excel by exalting the things that make you stand out.

I always stood out in high school. I was the girl who excitedly raised her hand first to answer a question. I was also the one who was in every club and activity and defined myself by my jam-packed schedule. The idea that girls are meant to blend in to achieve

Me and Digi agent Seth Rappaport with some mini merch at DigiFest Toronto

popularity never occurred to me. I was ambitious, hungry, and creative, and my blatant ambition made me disliked by most girls in my school.

Especially by one girl in particular. Her name was Katie (her name was not really Katie) and for whatever reason, I was pretty sure she didn't like me. She always had a snide comment about me, and a vague threat, but only when other people were around. It was frustrating, but I tried not to think about it too much. Everyone's going through something.

There was a party being thrown by a guy in my tenth-grade class. His name was Chuckie and he was that nice guy in high school who somehow can be friends with every single person. I got my hopes up. Way, way too up.

The number-one rule for a party is to dress appropriately, and I planned on being literally Cinderella. Carrie Bradshaw was shaping my wardrobe, and I wanted everyone to know it. I picked out a Betsey Johnson tutu skirt, covered in cherries, and pointy-toe stiletto shoes. None of the other girls owned a pair yet, as far as I knew.

I was so happy with how I looked, and excited about the party. My mom dropped me off in front, I knocked on the door, with my biggest, most pleasing smile plastered on my face, and was greeted by . . . Katie. She was wearing sweatpants and an Old Navy sweater. "Why are you here?" she asked. "And what in the *world* are you wearing?"

Some of Katie's friends came to see what was going on, and they all started laughing and calling me names. I mean okay *maybe* I was overdressed, but this was soul crushing. Clearly they knew better than I did that I didn't belong here.

"Chuckie invited me, he's my friend, too," I said.

"That's too bad, because I'm not letting you in here." Katie's eyes dared me to question her.

Me in 2012 as the BlackBerry spokesperson

"This isn't your party, you can't not let me in."

"Watch me!"

Katie stood in the doorway, her friends behind her. It was useless. I walked back out to the street and the girls clapped while I called my mom and told her to come back to get me. They taunted me from the doorway and windows until she got there. It was humiliating.

Teen girls made me miserable in high school, but now in my adulthood they've made me a Selfie Made CEO. I don't hold a grudge. I'm too busy for that. I love my job and love giving teens a "best day of your life" experience.

At every event I produce, I see girls that remind me of myself. DigiTour has given me a chance to be a teen again, and it's so much more fun the second time around. Why? Because I now understand that the opinions of other people don't have to mean anything to me if I don't let them. I have an excruciating amount of empathy for the frustrating and tumultuous experience of being a young girl. The pain, the fear, the hormones—they don't have to define you.

Not many years after that terrible party, I became the spokesperson for BlackBerry. I was in national TV commercials, print ads, and—my favorite—on billboards. One day I received a Facebook request from someone I sort of remembered from high school, so I accepted. It was Katie. She'd moved to New York, and her apartment looked right out on a forty-foot billboard of my face.

I'd completely forgotten about the incident, but when I read her message, I vividly remembered that day, and it all rushed back to me . . . for like two seconds. And then I laughed, and wrote, "Guess I'll be at all your parties, huh?"

I deleted that, and wrote, "It's nice to hear from you!" and left it at that. Karmic revenge already came in the form of a Godzilla-size Meridith; I didn't have to rub it in her face!

Oh, and the best part? There was a quote from me on that billboard: "I'm about action, not distraction."

I found my confidence, but it didn't come without some hard moments and bruised feelings. Finding your confidence online can be equally challenging. People can be mean and jealous. If you decide to post content and stand out, no matter what, I guarantee you will have haters and trolls.

Everyone is going through something, and for some people, it's hard to see their peers doing better than they are. These haters want to take their target down a few pegs. It's a knee-jerk reaction, emphasis on *jerk*.

Don't ever let a bully take away your hopes and dreams, whether that's offline or online. Why would you give a bully that power? I can't say it won't sting when you get negative comments, because it will, but you have two choices: you can let it bother you or you can let it go. Those are literally, seriously, truly, 100 percent for certain and certified, the only two choices. So pick one.

DO YOU

Chris and I were sitting in a super-fancy conference room in Los Angeles, meeting with the biggest event promoters in the world.

The promoters were interested in working with us, but had some questions about our business model. These aren't exactly stuffy people—they're used to spending their time with old-school musicians. But still, DigiTour was a new kind of puzzle for them, one they couldn't quite figure out.

This was a major moment for us. This company produced the world's greatest events, concerts, and festivals, and they were considering partnering with us on a new tour. Working with them would take our business into the stratosphere. DigiTour was doing great; we were fresh off another tour, and itching to do something bigger. These were the people that could make that happen.

And to top it all off, we had a new idea. A bigger, bolder, and crazier idea than they realized.

I stood up to make our presentation and thankfully this time, my PowerPoint worked. On their display wall popped up some of Digi's most successful acts: Pentatonix, Caspar Lee, Allstar Weekend, Tyler Ward, The Gregory Brothers. The pictures kept coming, piling up on top of each other.

"What we're proposing," I said, as the pictures kept coming, "is to totally change the way live events are put together. Social media has created new rules for how stars engage with their fans, and these events need to keep up with the trends."

"Change in what way?" one of the promoters asked.

"Change as in, I want to put every single one of the acts that just appeared on this screen all together for one live festival. That's fifty acts, on one stage."

There were noticeable chuckles. I thought about that party I was laughed out of. But I wasn't a timid little girl anymore, I was a Selfie Made CEO! Let them laugh, the laugh of the uninformed!

"Look, I get it," I said. "This is a big undertaking. But I can show you the numbers. It can work. We can make this happen and it will be a huge success. Let's do this! Go big or go home!"

"Meridith, we love you guys, we love DigiTour, but this is nuts. There's too much that can go wrong; fifty acts means fifty problems. Let's just get one headliner, a couple opening acts, and call it a day. No need to reinvent the wheel here."

But they were missing the point. We were reinventing the wheel, and that's what made it so exciting.

The promoters kept up with the hemming and hawing, and it became clear we were going to have some "creative differences." Eventually, Chris and I made silent eye contact. It was time to go. We politely declined a partnership.

"Where would you guys even be able to pull off an event like that?" one of them asked me on the way out.

"The heart of New York City. If we can make it there, we can make it anywhere!" I smiled wide, like I was in a musical. *DigiTour: The Musical!*

On the elevator ride out, Chris gave me a perplexed look. "New York?"

"What?"

"Why did you have to tell him New York? It's going to be a nightmare to pull that off!"

"We'll be fine," I said. "What's the worst that could happen?"

Trevor Moran A True OG

Trevor Moran has had a lot of lives on social media; it's hard to believe he's still a teen.

When I first met Trevor, O2L was brand-new, and he was just discovering who he is. He was the baby of the group, even though when they formed, he had the biggest channel. His Apple Store

Me and Trevor going tux shopping for a tour photo shoot, 2014

videos were just the beginning of his story.

Trevor is the life of the party, wherever he goes. He loves to make people laugh, but he also isn't afraid to show what's underneath the laughter. Underneath it all, Trevor has a good heart, and I love him to pieces!

A lot of social media stars gain fans and lose them just as quickly. Trevor, on the other hand, has seen his fan base turn over and start anew. As he grew up and became more comfortable with himself, his audience grew, too.

There is such a thing as longevity in social media. You can have it, too.

You've been on social for how long?

Ten years.

How did you start?

I found my dad's laptop in the garbage, tried to put it back together with tape, got it to work, and started filming myself. I learned how to use Windows Movie Maker and put on voice effects and filters. I was eight years old at the time. Even if I got ten views I'd be like, that's more people than you can fit into a car. Now I think of how many views I get and that's bigger than a whole freakin' stadium! People started noticing when I was eleven and made videos dancing into the Apple Store. I would open Photo Booth on their computers and start dancing. No one asked me to leave. And once it went viral, people in the stores would say "it's the Apple Store Kid" when I'd walk in and head over to the computer. People thought the dances were choreographed, but it was all on the fly.

What were your videos called?

Apple Store Dance to "Song Title" (no clickbait—you get what you click).

How did you turn from Apple Store Kid into Trevor Moran?

I was trying to upload other videos, trying to vlog and do skits, but the viewers hated it and all the comments were "Go back to Apple Store, do what you're known for." It was so sad. I would get a lot of hate if I didn't post a video in the Apple Store.

Then I auditioned for *The X Factor*. Shortly after I met members of what later became known as O2L, Our Second

Life: Connor Franta, Sam Pottorff, Kian Lawley, Rick Dillon, and Jc Caylen.

How did O2L take off and grow from ten thousand collective subscribers to what became "YouTube's Super Group"?

Consistency of uploading every day. It took about six months until we were getting fifty thousand views per video. After a year we were really growing—we were blowing up.

How have you been able to maintain your relevance?

It's all about creating a personal connection with people who watch you. You'll get different waves of people who follow you. For me, the more time goes on, the more real I get. I don't have time to be fake. After O2L ended, I came out, I wore makeup, I changed. Some of the original O2L fans who followed the collab channel because we were "cute boys" unsubscribed/ unfollowed. I may have lost a couple thousand, but I gained so many more. Being real and allowing for fan turnover is what allowed me to stay around for so long.

> Authenticity is what's going to keep you relevant.

Is your audience today different than your Apple Store audience?

In a way, yes. That was eight or nine years ago, some of those people could have a family now. But some people have come up to me at events and said they have been watching that long.

Are you afraid of ever becoming irrelevant?

No, because I have so many loyal people that I know will be there for a long time. And I believe in myself and I am a hard worker. And if five years come and I can't make a living talking in front of a white wall anymore, there are so many other things I would try. I've been in this game so long I feel like I'm thirty-five, and I look in the mirror and slap my face and say, "You're freakin' nineteen!"

What do you think about new platforms making stars? Is there a rivalry among platforms?

I see YouTubers get mad at Musers. I see nothing wrong with Musers and I don't see how people can hate on the new kids. I applaud these kids for being so young and hopping on the newest trends. I see nothing wrong with Musers or YouNowers. I want to see who the smart ones are. I want to see how they maximize their careers. I love Baby Ariel and Weston Koury.

Do you feel pressure to share everything?

I keep my personal life very separate. At the same time I'm not afraid of being an open book. I'll tell them whatever they want to know. I was hiding that I was gay for so long; it was my management and people on my team who held me back.

How do you make money?

1. Brand deals/partnerships
2. Ad revenue on YouTube
3. Song sales/streaming

Advice for someone starting out?

1. Don't try to be someone that's already been; nobody likes a wannabe. Create your own brand.
2. Don't move to Los Angeles until you're ready.
3. The only person who's going to take you further is yourself.
4. Merch: take your time. I never did that well because I rushed in with bad designs. Why didn't it sell? Oh, because it was ugly.

FINDING YOUR TRIBE

Since neither Chris nor I had a traditional background in producing live events, we were often making things up as we went along. It just so happens that by doing so, we were making up the rules for how social media talent goes on tour.

We started booking all the talent, and everyone was definitely on board. Basically, when DigiTour calls and says the top fifty social media stars are converging onto one stage for a one-night-only event, everyone wants in.

We also wanted to feature some up-and-coming acts, too, so we reached out to a band that had DM'ed us on Twitter. They'd heard about the event and wanted to participate. They even offered to cover their own travel. They called themselves O2L, aka Our Second Life, and there were five of them: Connor Franta, Trevor Moran, Kian Lawley, Jc Caylen, Ricky Dillon, and Sam Pottorff.

At the time they had about two hundred thousand subscribers, which wasn't bad at all, except when compared to the other talent we had onstage, who all had millions of subs. But we took a chance!

The fest plans were going supersmoothly, almost too smoothly, except for one teeny, tiny, overlooked detail: I never made hotel arrangements for my fifty YouTubers and their plus-ones and -twos!

I flew to New York a week before the event, and did what seemed the most logical thing to do: I walked door-to-door into a handful of boutique hotels and asked them if they had seventy rooms for the following week.

The reactions this elicited ranged from laughter to anger. A few of the hotel managers thought I was pranking them. One started looking

for a hidden camera. But when I set out to do
something I don't come home without getting
it done, and so there I was, trying my best to
negotiate a deal on a huge block of rooms, with
only six days until my guests arrived.

*Me and O2L during a photoshoot
for tour at the Santa Monica Pier,
2014*

Luckily I found a spot: Pod 39. A hip hotel
on Thirty-ninth Street with a Ping-Pong table,
taqueria, and rooms that literally could not be
smaller; the name of the hotel was accurate. Each *pod* was basically a tour bus
bunk. In fact, the rooms were so small it was almost a novelty. At least that's
how I played it off.

The show went off smashingly. Tickets sold out almost as soon as they
went on sale, and all our acts had a fantastic time. And the biggest surprise
of the night? Our Second Life was hands down the most popular act of the
night. We started working all the members into upcoming tours.

By the next year, O2L was one of the biggest acts on social media. We
decided to put together a headlining tour for them.

"We need to come up with a way to surprise your fans with the tour
news," I told them. We brainstormed for a while and came up with the
perfect idea: we'd wrap them up in gift wrap, and then they could unwrap
themselves onstage, and reveal U.S. TOUR T-shirts underneath! It was just days
before Christmas, and who wouldn't want to unwrap O2L under their tree?

"OMG, Meridith, you're giving me anxiety," said Trevor. Trevor had a flair
for the dramatic. "I'm claustrophobic just thinking about it."

"Trevor, you'll have paper touching your body for like thirty seconds, and
then you'll take it off. The fans will lose their minds."

I got a reluctant eye roll and on we moved!

Me and O2L backstage on tour

As predicted, the crowd went nuts. As the guys tore off their wrapping paper, I turned on a snow machine. It was pure YouTube magic. When we did put tix on sales the tour sold out the same day. It was a tour producer's dream. We were on a roll.

Out of all the tours I've produced, O2L's was the one I was the most hands-on for. I creatively directed nearly every aspect. I took the guys to improvisation classes and offered my own ideas (I can be funny sometimes). I sat with them in each rehearsal and we came up with each segment, including a grand finale where the guys did a choreographed dance. Now keep in mind, they're not a band. They were a *vlogging* group. But they were the heartthrobs and it-boys and the girls loved seeing them. As a former boy-band obsessive myself, I explained that having them break into a dance would literally be so epic girls may actually pass out.

Out of the group, Connor was the business-focused member. He was ultracompetitive and always thinking of ways to continue to fan the fan base. Even today his accomplishments in business are impressive: a subscription coffee line, a record label, two books, and a clothing line in Urban Outfitters. He's a smart guy.

Connor put together a song for the show, with a producer who was unknown at the time, named Charlie Puth. Yeah, Connor has good instincts.

The song was great and the boys danced, dressed in bananas suits, and sprayed the audience with Silly String. From top to bottom the show was extremely entertaining. The fans loved it and I was proud because *I felt I was a part of it*. That's what it's all about.

Lauren Godwin — Musical.ly's Favorite Comedienne

Tell me how you grew your audience. How long did it take?

I came across Musical.ly: the hand motions everyone was doing caught my attention. Then I stumbled across the comedy section. I really like acting and gave it a try. I filmed a video and the next day it was featured. That video received two hundred thousand likes. Growing an audience took about eighteen months, but after the feature I grew about five thousand followers per day. Another thing that helped was I was on the platform early. At fifty thousand followers I was crowned!

What's your most important platform?

Musical.ly. It took me awhile to translate my audience from Musical.ly to my other platforms.

You have a definite comedic edge to your content. What made you start to introduce characters/ wigs/props? Do you think that helped? Would you recommend others starting out try that, too?

I always go out with my family for Halloween. We have a big bin in the garage with wigs, etc. So one day I decided to just use them and create characters. Other people have also used this approach in their videos.

Top five pieces of advice for someone just starting out?

1. Trending hashtags.
2. Good lighting/bright colors.
3. Exaggerated facial expressions.
4. Props.
5. Most importantly have fun with it.

When did you realize it was becoming a job?

When I was getting offered to do Live.ly and app promotions.

When did you first realize you had supporters?

I remember I was at a social media event for another person and someone came up to me in line and said, "You're that person from Musical.ly." I only had ten thousand followers. I didn't think someone would notice me at that point.

Who do you look up to?

Liza Koshy on YouTube.

How do you make $?

- Live.ly users send you gifts.
- App promos. Don't dilute your page. Don't do too much. I focus on bigger brand deals.
- Touring.
- Merch.

Flattery will get you everywhere. Try to get the attention of your icons by reviewing their work, sharing their new videos, and remixing their work. Congratulate them on new project releases or special days. Everyone loves being complimented—make it work for you!

Selfie Made Mode:

- ▷ Figure out what makes you stand out, and amplify it!
- ▷ To defeat a troll, you must ignore a troll.
- ▷ Look for like-minded people.

Consistency

POST LIKE A MILLION PEOPLE ARE WATCHING.

In the beginning of DigiTour no one really knew what it was yet. However, when building a brand (whether a company like DigiTour or your own personal lifestyle brand as a social media star) you need to think *big*.

People pick up on how you view something. If you see yourself as a small channel that doesn't matter, that's how you'll be perceived. It should become your mission to go out and spread the word of what you're creating and be confident about it.

For DigiTour, Chris and I would go to teen concerts and movies that catered to our audience, and pass out flyers with info on Digi and our next show. If there was an event we needed to be at, we were there.

Whenever we met a prospective fan, we always led with the same line: "We are the world's first social media tour." This one line was our elevator pitch. Do you know what your elevator pitch is for your brand? If you have to describe your brand to someone in the time it takes for an elevator to go from the ground floor to the fifth floor, what would you say?

Our pitch changed as our business changed. Our elevator pitch became: "We are the largest producer of live events featuring social media stars." And pretty soon we didn't need an elevator pitch anymore because people we met already knew who we were. That was always the goal. You should start out on your journey believing that it *will* happen. You *will* create something that *will* make a dent in pop culture.

Even if your current audience is comprised of only friends and family, it is crucial to post like you have the demand of an engaged following. Treating your social media as though a million people are watching will help you post more consistently, which can be difficult at first. However, with consistency, the "I don't know what to say or post" feeling will fade and you'll get into a rhythm.

You can't count on a viral moment, but you can give yourself the best shot at growing. Being active will improve your chances. It's not rocket science: the more often you post, the better chance you have of one of your posts going viral.

Social is a source of entertainment. If you're posting an Insta Story every day, people watch, and you're at the top of their minds, and literally at the top of their feed, and soon the people watching may just come to look forward to your posts. But if you ghost for two weeks because you had a cold, an exam, and a fight with your best friend, people will forget about your content and glom on to someone else who's posting twice as much.

To be clear, just as important as posting enough is not posting too much: aka spamming. Spamming is a no-no and it's the fastest way to get someone to unfollow you. We all have those friends who post Insta Stories with thirty pics, each of different angles of their food. Don't be that person. You don't want your feed taken over by someone posting pic after pic, and your fans don't want it, either. Overposting is a rookie mistake and if you're reading this book, you're no longer a rookie.

SET A SCHEDULE

Whenever I'm helping a new creator map out a plan for growth, we start with a schedule. A social media schedule provides a solid foundation for growth. Consistency won't necessarily make you go viral, as many social stars can attest to. Take Blake Gray, for example. Before he went viral, he was just posting whenever he felt like it. Social wasn't a business for him before his viral moment, he was just having fun. But when the opportunity struck, he ran with it.

The easiest way to be consistent with your posting is to create a schedule. This schedule will be different for everyone, depending on your preferred platform and what your goals are in the social media realm.

Your schedule is for no one but you. It's not like homework. You won't get in trouble or fail a class for not handing it in. No one else will hold you to your schedule but you, because no one else stands to gain anything from your social media except you (and your followers!). If you're not the type of person who can stick to a schedule, then keep your schedule light! This book is for you; make it work around what works for you. But maybe you can push yourself to commit to your social media future and retrain your brain to stay on schedule.

I asked a bunch of DigiTour talent what their social media schedules were, calculated all the results, and put together this easy cheat-sheet example schedule. If you can keep on schedule, this mix will set you up for success:

Twitter: four times per day

Snapchat: four to six times per day

Instagram: two to three times per week

Instagram Story: two to four times per day

YouTube: once per week or every other week (ideal if you want to push video content but not required for starters)

YouNow or Live.ly: two to three times per week

Musical.ly: once or twice per day

Your schedule may be different depending on what your goals are, but that schedule will keep you on track with all your socials.

Here are some more sample schedules from your favorite stars:

TREVOR MORAN'S SCHEDULE:

Twitter: three to five times per day

Insta: once per day

Insta Story and Snap: five to ten times per day

LAUREN GODWIN'S SCHEDULE:

Musical.ly: I wake up every morning and film. It takes thirty minutes for one vid and I post seven per day.

Snap: two per day (mostly toward friends, but I'm very serious about streaks . . . stories not as often).

Live.ly: three times per week. Some months I set goals to go live every day.

DANIELLE COHN'S SCHEDULE:

Musical.ly: three times per day

Insta: once per day

Twitter: two to three times per day

Snap: five times per day

Flipagram: once per day

Mads Lewis Knows How To Engage

Mads is breaking out in the acting world on the popular web series *Chicken Girls*, but she still manages to be one of the realest, most down-to-earth girls in the game on her socials. And that's what being Selfie Made is all about! I asked Mads how she manages to engage with her fans, I mean her family, and here's what she had to say:

How did you get started?

When I was in sixth grade I started using Musical.ly, but I wasn't doing it with any goal in mind. I just liked the app and was having fun. They had a lot of comedy challenges and I love comedy. It was a place where I could be myself. If I was feeling silly or serious, whatever my mood was, I could express myself on Musical.ly more than I could on other apps.

What was your tipping point?

I started off with, like, one thousand followers, and I tried my best to get featured, but it didn't seem like it would ever happen. One day my mom told me I got featured and I didn't believe her, I thought she was messing with me, but then I looked and I was like, *what*?! After that first time, I got featured over and over again. Then I got crowned, and more people started following me. Musical.ly was very supportive, and they even invited me to their offices in Santa Monica.

How fast were your followers growing?

I had about five features before I got crowned, and when I got crowned I had about fifty thousand followers.

How did you get featured?

I always did the challenges, especially the comedy ones, and I think Musical.ly liked that my posts were so unique.

What's your advice on postings?

Do what makes you happy. Post when you want to post. If it makes you happy it'll make your followers happy. Be yourself. If people follow you on social and then they meet you in person and you act differently, that's a problem. Your social should be a real reflection of who you are, otherwise it won't work.

What's your relationship like with your fans?

I hate calling them fans, that's an "f" word to me. I call them family. They watch out for me, literally. When people comment, I like it immediately. They took the time to write something, I take the time to respond. Some social influencers have real ride-or-die fandoms, and some of these fandoms like to fight each other, but I tell my followers that if they don't like someone, keep it to themselves. That's the culture I've created with my fandom.

Is it overwhelming to be so suddenly famous?

I don't like the word "famous" either, to me that's another "f" word. I'd feel really silly referring to myself as "famous." I was using a social app and they thought I was funny and featured me. That's it. I try not to take myself too seriously. I'm not using social to get a high follower count, I'm using it to be social with people around the world. I'd rather have a handful of really strong supporters that I engage with all the time than a massive amount of followers I never interact with.

I do notice you're the top comment on a lot of people's posts.

I support all my friends. It's nice to see your friends comment on photos and I've met a lot of friends through social. I follow people because I like them, I don't care about how many followers they have. That doesn't really matter. Numbers don't change who you are.

What are your goals now?

I'm starting to act and I got cast on this show, *Chicken Girls*, which I really enjoy, so I want to become a bigger actor. And maybe a print model, like for fashion magazines. Oh, and I'm still trying to get verified on Instagram!

Selfie Made Mode:

▷ Be as consistent in your social media posting as I am consistent about using the word *consistent* in this (consistently awkward) sentence.

▷ Set a schedule.

▷ BE AUTHENTIC!

YouTube Speak

Earlier I talked about the YouTube ocean, and how difficult it can be to break into the biggest of the platforms.

And let me guess: you don't care, you're going for the big kahuna?

Or maybe you've already mastered another platform but it's time to make the switch?

Or you've been YouTubing since 2010 but need a brush-up on new ways to up your engagement?

No matter what your sitch, here are some specifics of what to look out for on YouTube. There are a lot of moving pieces here, and something that may seem small, like a thumbnail, is actually one of the most important parts of your video.

We'll just jump right in and go over everything you need to know to get your YouTube page in order.

THUMBNAILS

That tiny photo that appears next to a video file? That's a thumbnail, and it can be what gets your video clicked on . . . or what gets your video ignored. Make sure your thumbnails look good on both desktops and mobile, and experiment with them! Try a few different types of thumbnails and see what works for you.

Always make your thumbnails custom! Always! You can use graphic designers to make thumbnails for you, too. Is there someone you know who will help you? Maybe you trade services? (#collab)

If you're using a still photo from your video, use the most exciting, or the most confusing and perplexing. Remember: no clickbait. But you want people to *want* to click on it.

Create a border around your thumbnail to make it stand out. And try out some fake 3-D effects. Whatever you do, make sure the text matches the title. If it doesn't match, it will get fewer clicks.

Think about your thumbnail and set it up during your upload process, so it's there from your first view. If you try to update it afterward, it can take days, and sometimes weeks to change over!

TITLES

Make sure your title matches your content, and avoid ALL CAPS, and a lot. Of. Punc. Tu. A. Tion. Also, YouTube suggests you keep your title less than sixty characters.

All of your video titles should have the same style and capitalization, and put episode numbers at the end of the title (if there are episodes). Oh, and avoid profanity and being vulgar. I know, it's funny, but it will lead to fewer clicks.

Experiment before you upload a final title, and think of the title before you start the upload process so it's there from your first view!

DESCRIPTIONS

The beginning of your description should match your title, and the ending should be your social media callouts. Check out Google Trends and YouTube Search reports to see what keywords will lead people to your videos and learn, learn, learn.

http:// is required for links. Don't make a rookie mistake!

Think about your description and set it up during your upload process so it's there from your first view!

And most importantly: use this chance to engage! Ask questions of your fans in the description!

COMMENTING

Use the comments section to interact with fans on new videos, to drive engagement, especially in the first twenty-four hours. Ask and answer questions, be self-deprecating, and tell fans on other platforms that you're jumping into the comments on YouTube so they better be on the lookout.

Screenshot your favorite comments and put them on other platforms to show fans that you're actually reading them. Use comments to drive engagement to older videos, too.

UPLOAD TIME

Make sure to upload at a time when your fans are awake.

To start, try midafternoon on weekdays and midmorning on weekends. Examine your results once you've put up your first month of videos. When is your peak watch time? Are you gaining a lot of fans in another country? If so, perhaps you adjust your upload time.

Most importantly, make sure it's a convenient time for you so that you can keep up with your schedule.

END SCREENS

Use your end screen to point to other videos or playlists, ask fans to subscribe, or promote other channels or links.

Think about your end screen and set it up during your upload process so it's there from your first view.

SHOUT-OUTS

Constantly remind fans to subscribe, like, and comment on your video. Tell fans how much you appreciate them watching and shout-out your new fans.

Give clues about your next video and get fans excited. Remind them about your upload times so they can schedule it.

Ask questions! This is a helpful way to get ideas for new videos.

Start a dialogue in the comments. Reward fans by answering some of their questions in the next video.

CHANNEL TRAILER

Create a short, fun trailer that represents you, your channel, and what fans should expect.

If you don't have much uploaded yet, then just talk to the audience and tell them why you're awesome and why you'd like them to give your channel a chance.

What's Your YouTuber Niche?

They say the riches are in the niches! Not sure what kind of content you want to create? The answer is to be specific! There are a lot of recurring themes on YouTube, and usually that's because they're the types of themes that attract a lot of eyeballs.

Here's some of the top niches on YouTube:

Gamer: Dedicates content to reviewing, playing, and commenting on video games.

Beauty Guru: A self-proclaimed expert, usually dedicating vids to tutorials on certain makeup and style looks and trends as well as reviewing products.

BookTuber: All about the books and discussing their latest reads.

DIYer: A booming category of influencer dedicated to "Do It Yourself" activities, from decorating your room to making your own slime. The range is wide but always includes crafting and creativity.

Lifecaster: At its core, someone who broadcasts their life and creates entertainment through infusing mundane day-in-the-life activities with humor, personality, or their own unique POV. This is my fav category, because it is a new concept that belongs to the internet world and Gen Z.

Vlogger: Specifically creates videos documenting daily activities.

Storyteller: Tells elaborate stories to viewers, usually on hot topics. This is a new category. Tana Mongeau is a great example.

· · ·

Selfie Made Mode:

Find your niche!

On the
Road Again,
with
DigiTour

IF YOU'RE AN ARTIST,
NOT HAVING A
FOLLOWING MEANS
NOT HAVING A CAREER.

Chris and I started DigiTour by going out and finding a tour bus, and although I don't get on every tour bus anymore, I try to go as often as I can.

Being on a tour bus with a DigiTour lineup of the coolest kids on the internet is a very special kind of experience. It's one of those memories that lingers with you.

Going on tour and getting my hands into every facet of running a tour taught me a lot of useful, long-term-memory kind of information. For example, on a tour bus, the middle bunk is the best. The top bunk can be wobbly and the bottom bunk is on foot level.

The main thing I learned, the most important thing, is that by the end of a tour, the talent and the crew feel like a big family. And just like every family, everyone has their roles. On every tour I've been on, from the very first to the very last, I've wound up being called Mom by the talent. It's a moniker I cherish.

There are a lot of behind-the-scenes people that go into putting a show together. They're known as the crew. When Chris and I first started, it was just us doing the jobs of ten different people. We didn't have the resources to pay for a whole crew, and had to make do. But we hired proper staff as soon as we were able, because having the right people around allowed us to focus on bigger-picture problems.

Still, when we hired a new person, I would watch what they did, and take mental notes. The better I understood what everyone did and how everything worked, the better my future shows would be, and the more successful my business would become.

Ideally, in a professional crew you'll have:

1. **Tour manager:** The boss on the road. It is the tour manager's responsibility to manage the rest of the crew, to make sure everything runs smoothly, safely, and on time, and they're usually the person who handles any major issues. Tour managers are also in charge of "advancing" to each venue; in other words, the tour manager is in touch with each venue and gives them all the details of the upcoming show, and a list of all of the things that are needed (security, catering, loading in/loading out gear, guest list, etc., etc., ad nauseam).

2. **Stage manager:** Most of the talent sees the stage manager as the person on the side of the stage who is making sure they're ready to go on. Stage managers also handle loading in/out of the venue with all of the tour's gear. For a music tour, this can include drum kit, guitars, amps, DJ equipment, as well as any sets, props, and signage. For DigiTour, our stage manager has also had to contend with a big, heavy, old snow machine, and hamster balls big enough for our talent to fit inside. Anything that happens in the wings or on the stage, the stage manager has an eye on it.

3. **Talent wrangler:** This role doesn't always exist on the smaller tours and sometimes is handled by a combo of the PA and the stage manager. When this role is included their sole job is to make sure the talent is where they need to be, and that they're taken care of.

4. **PA:** Production assistant—*technically* the lowest on the totem pole of the crew, but often one of the most important. PAs run around and make sure the signs are hung, pick up catering and/or order food for talent,

support the tour manager in his/her many duties, and help with coordinating the meet & greet.

5. **VIP coordinator:** Meet & greets are an important part of DigiTour events, and these guys make sure the experience runs smoothly. They set up the step and repeat, which is a backdrop with the DigiTour logo that makes for a great setting for fan pics. Then they check in the VIP ticket holders, distribute goodies (posters, laminates), and help take pictures, move the line along, and ensure we start the show on time. If the meet & greet runs late, the show starts late. Most venues have a curfew, and if you go over it, there are hefty fines.

6. **Merch seller:** This person is responsible for shipping merch, selling merch, counting merch at the beginning and end of each show (aka taking inventory), and accounting for the money. Usually the venue takes a percentage. For an event like DigiTour, each of the talent can have their own merch, which needs to be accounted for separately, so there is a lot of math involved here.

7. **Talent:** These are the people out onstage, making the magic, night after night, whether they're sick, tired, plague ridden, whatever. Actually, no plague please, DigiTour Zombie Edition is not my style.

MEET & GREET

Sure, you want to come to DigiTour to see the show, but you also want to come for the meet & greet!

Meet & greets are so essential to understanding the connection between creators and their supporters that I make every new employee who starts at

DigiTour work one of them. The meet & greet is when a fan's internet dreams come true. It's the culmination of many hours of spamming to get noticed, entering contests, dreaming of a DM, and hours and hours of consuming their fav's content.

When you're a social media star and you have an active fan base, your supporters feel like they know you . . . because they do! Each day you post ten-plus pieces (sometimes more) across platforms. They see your friends, your house, and even your food. Fans take note of emotions you share via tweets or video rants. They're there for you when you're feeling alone, and they support you when the haters come out.

By design, meet & greets are brief, quick-and-go things. That means the most important part of it is the photo. The goal of a great m&g photo is to capture in that quick flash *all of the feels!* It needs to look like you know each other.

When I was ten and eleven, I was obsessed with the band Hanson. Okay, specifically, Taylor Hanson. You know, the "MMMBop" band. Le sigh. I would rip out pages featuring their pictures from *Tiger Beat* magazine and tape them to my wall. I listened to their CD on repeat so many times that it warped the disc. Just thinking about it makes me love Spotify even more.

Naturally, during all this CD warping, I was pining and opining my absolute love for Taylor Hanson. Meeting Taylor, in person, in front of my face, like literally looking at him? That was never in the realm of possibility for me. Maybe he did VIP events somewhere, but that kind of information wasn't making its way to my part of Connecticut.

For Gen Z, the timeless experience of a first-celeb crush has dramatically changed. There's unlimited access to your crush through their social platforms. And getting a VIP ticket and meeting your fav is now a very real possibility.

In many ways, this was the whole point of what Chris and I were trying to do with DigiTour, and why we knew it would work. I understood the power of the emotion behind that celeb crush because I had experienced it myself, and in some ways, I still experience it. My love for Taylor Hanson will always be a part of me. Sorry Chris. (#notsorry)

Social media stars connect with their fans in a way that previous celebrities were never able to do. That much was obvious to me. But it was also obvious to me that having so much more access to a star meant that the rules of being a star were completely changing. When fans interact with you day after day, an emotional bond develops. Stars and fans, influencers and supporters, you can't spend so much time getting to know someone without meeting them face-to-face. Not with Gen Z.

Once I understood this, meet & greets became a really important part of my business. When a fan meets their fav IRL, it's like they're running into a best friend that moved out of town.

I didn't ever think Taylor Hanson would know my name. Now, many supporters think, or even *expect* (for good reason!) that it is possible for their favs to recognize them. And very often, they do!

For an influencer, meet & greets are a terrific way to make a fan for life.

STRIKE A POSE

One thing I did not expect when we started doing meet & greets was how prepared supporters were for their picture poses! A few of the more popular choices:

1. **The Stage Kiss:** Banned by some events, and some talent's girlfriends!
   The creator puts their lips on their thumb, presses their face to yours,

and makes it look (to the camera and surrounding observers) like you're actually kissing. My teenage self would have wanted a photo of me kissing one of the Hanson brothers blown up into a poster on my wall!

2. **The Run and Jump:** This controversial pose has also had its fair share of bannings. The reason is simple: safety. Not all the creators are musclemen. On more than one occasion a fan has run and jumped, wrapped their legs around them, and instead of the romantic movie effect both of them have tumbled to the ground with a few bruises and a backache.

3. **The Prom Shot:** This is a safe bet and usually will not get declined. It's the standing-spoon as I like to call it and either the supporter gets in front of the creator who then wraps his/her arms around them in a traditional prom pose or sometimes they switch it up and the supporter opts to be the outside standing-spoon cuddling the creator from behind.

4. **The Piggyback:** This one is a fav but also a potential safety hazard. Similar to the run and jump, this pose involves either the creator jumping on the supporter's back or vice versa. I've witnessed many creators asking to retire this one as a few times they collapsed from the impact.

5. **The Head-in-Hands-Lie-on-Ground Pose:** This pose is exactly as it sounds. No one is taking themselves too seriously here. Everyone gets on the floor, lying on their stomach, and then everyone rests their face on their hands, usually with a MASSIVE cheesy smile. This pose shouts, "We are basically best friends!"

6. **The Head-to-Head Pose:** This pose is when both the creator and supporter hold hands and then gently touch foreheads. It implies a deep connection. It definitely falls into the "we look like we're in love" category of pose and it is one of the fan favs.

WITH GREAT POWER . . .

Our first international DigiFest took place in London.

It was a killer lineup: Zoella, Lilly Singh, Connor Franta, and Troye Sivan. We sold out the Hammersmith Apollo: that's four thousand seats. You know what that means? Four thousand supporters, piling in to see talent who rarely (if ever) came to their city. And another few hundred who piled into the lobby of our hotel and camped out. Somehow they found us! We politely asked the hotel manager at 2 A.M. if they could escort our adoring and adored (but very loud) UK fans out so we could sleep, but they all had booked rooms, too. Now that's next-level dedication!

Preshow, we had our meet & greet set up. Nearly six hundred fans lined up, our biggest meet & greet yet. That was fine by us; that just meant more happy fans! My team was in position, and ready to start moving.

Our show was supposed to start at seven, and it became clear at six thirty that this m&g was going to be running late. If a m&g runs late, the concert runs late. If the concert runs late, we won't load out of the venue on time, and we'll incur penalty fees.

The venue was giving me a lot of pressure to get things moving, but I was in a tough spot. The talent was really delighted to meet their international fans, and they were having a lot of fun talking to them. Typically each fan might get about thirty seconds, tops, but these fans were getting a few minutes each. I didn't want to rush this process, but we were clearly not going to finish in the allotted time.

Trying to keep it together, my team and I huddled and tried to think of a way to pause the m&g and resume it midshow. We had gotten through 75 percent but still had about a hundred and fifty fans waiting in the queue.

The venue put their foot down and said if we didn't end the m&g and start the show, they would. It was a terrible feeling. I had to go break some hearts.

I grabbed a bullhorn and stood up on a chair. "Hi, everyone!" I yelled. "We need to get the concert started. Don't worry, if you haven't gone through the line yet you will get a hole punch in your VIP laminate. Midshow we will make an announcement from stage and reorganize the m&g for those with the hole punch to meet the talent."

There were no boos, and no tears (of sadness, there were plenty of tears of joy), so it seemed as though the crisis had been averted.

Midshow, we did exactly what we'd said we were going to do, and announced from the stage the new m&g location for those remaining one hundred and fifty fans. The crew got ready and the talent took their places in front of the step, but then something not so great happened. The fans lined up. But instead of a hundred and fifty people, there were six hundred again.

I was crushed. What was I going to do? Some clever girls had gone to the local hardware store, bought a hole punch, and now every VIP had punched their passes and lined up for a second go. When everyone figured out what was happening, the waterworks really started. There was nothing I could do. I just had to pull the plug on the m&g.

When I announced we were shutting it down, I made about one hundred of my customers cry. Even some of their parents were teary eyed. One dad turned red as a lobster and started hyperventilating. I ran up to him to see what I could do.

"I brought my girls here from Belgium, and all they wanted was to meet their hero. I came so close to giving that to them, and now it won't happen." Wow was that devastating. I told him to grab his girls and I took them to meet their favorites. At least I could make things right with this one family.

There are always hard choices to be made when you're in charge, and sometimes you have to make a call knowing someone will get upset, no matter what decision you make. All you can do is try to be responsible with your position of power. If it was up to me, I would never want an unhappy fan, but that's not realistic. It happens and it's how you deal with it and care about it that can take you from Selfie Made to a Selfie Made CEO.

COLLABORATION STATION

The tour bus was one giant moving collaboration station.

As the shows went on, all of our talent's social numbers started climbing exponentially. That's because each of the talent has a slightly different audience. By taking the stage together, and posting pictures together on the bus, they're combining audiences, and thus, each experiencing growth.

When Musical.ly was brand-new I received a call from their president, Alex Hofmann. He introduced himself and his app, which today would need no introduction but at that point was only starting to break through.

"I've been hearing about your Musers, but I don't know much about them," I said. "I don't know if they're ready for DigiTour yet."

Alex assured me they were. He ran through his pitch, sharing info on his app's growth, user engagement, and who his biggest stars were. He was clearly passionate about his business, and he reminded me of myself. I figured it was worth a shot.

We had just finished two big festivals and had another event coming up in Houston. I suggested to Alex that we have his biggest talent come out to Texas for a test run. That was Baby Ariel.

The other talent on the bill in Houston were not familiar with this girl, or her platform, and it took some getting used to. However, when she got on the stage, the audience definitely knew her. She ended up getting the loudest audience reaction of the whole show. She nailed her performance, became a fan favorite, and before long her Musical.ly fame was transferring to other platforms, too.

Me, Baby Ariel, and Nash @ PTTOW! 2016

DigiTour helped shine a light on Baby Ariel, and introduce her to a community of actively touring creators. In a world where being an influencer is more common every day, talent needs ways to stand out. Going on DigiTour or being featured at Playlist Live or being talked about by Messy Monday shows relevance. Following + recognition in the community = relevance.

When we produced Jack & Jack's first headline tour we were able to help them brand themselves more "music" than the previous m&g tour they were on. They didn't want to be known only as part of a social media pack of cute boys; they wanted to step out on their own. That tour helped them garner the buzz and recognition they needed to be individuals (with the same name).

Me, Jack & Jack at the premiere of the documentary we shot together (Photo courtesy of Getty images; photographer, Chelsea Lauren)

After the tour, Chris and I produced a Jack & Jack documentary. When I say *produced*, I mean we put the whole thing together; it was just the two of us and the two Jacks. We wanted to show the world that we could do anything. We didn't need music studios, we didn't need big-event planners, and we didn't need a Hollywood studio to make a movie!

We hired a videographer, flew out to their hometown of Omaha, Nebraska, and filmed some footage of their school, friends, and family. Our goal was to make a movie about how these two kids got so popular on Vine.

During our shooting, Jack & Jack went on another tour, and were nominated for a Teen Choice Award. Their stars were rising, and we caught it all on camera.

Before the documentary even premiered, we earned back the money we'd spent on it, just from preorders alone. Why am I telling you this? Because you can do it all yourself. Every single thing I've written about in this book, you can do yourself. You want to be a social media star because you want to create content, right? And eventually, you want to leverage your social following and use it to create long-form content, like movies, TV shows, or books? Being Selfie Made does not just apply to social media, it applies to all forms of media, and all forms of business.

HIT THE ROAD!

Have I convinced you touring is a good idea? Or did you already know that? Now comes the big question: how do you get invited or booked on a tour, at an event, or even put together your own meet-up?

There's no magic number of followers you need to go meet supporters IRL. Oftentimes creators start by attending events as a guest, in order to get a sense of what it's all about. There's a certain excitement at events where attendees go into creator-watching mode (it's like going to the zoo or going whale watching) and they want to spot as many people as they can. The heightened energy helps even smaller creators get the chance to interact with supporters, make an impression, take pics, sign things, and this has a positive effect on your social growth.

If you can find an opportunity to get invited to a tour, you should take it. At any level of following you'll see a positive effect. Until you've built a monetizable audience, all appearances and touring should be seen as promotional and a way to grow. What you'll get out of it is tenfold what you could possibly negotiate as a performance fee.

Start off by just buying a ticket and showing up for an event. It's a relatively inexpensive way to start, and a great way to litmus test your budding popularity in a sea of social media fans. DigiTour produces tours throughout the year across the U.S., Playlist Live is a twice-per-year event (Orlando and D.C.) that is full of creators and fans, and VidCon happens once a year in Anaheim. It is a bit bigger and more corporate but even more flooded with fans. The social stars at these events can be hard to connect with, so just like Allstar Weekend used a Jonas Brothers concert line to make new fans, you can make new fans and test your own recognition in the crowd. At VidCon 2017, many of the new and exploding Musers who weren't booked to appear at the event (but showed up anyway) were kicked out by security because they were creating mobs!

Imagine coming home and having to explain to your parents what happened.

"You got kicked out of VidCon?"

"Yes."

"Why?"

"Because the fans liked me so much it started to create mass chaos."

"Oh. Good job, I guess!"

I don't know if there's a better reason to be kicked out of somewhere.

Once you know you have some recognition and can get fans to show up for an event, you have a few options:

1. Organize your own free meet-up in your city. Even better, round up a few

of your friends who also have a following and team up. Get a crowd to show up and then brag about it. This gets our attention at DigiTour and others will take note, too.

2. Take to social. Ask your supporters to tweet a hashtag to get our attention, something like #yournameondigi. We have booked a lot of talent who came to us this way. Use your social and support from your fans to create a buzz that DigiTour can see.

3. Connect with talent who are slightly bigger than you. If you can align with someone already going on tour and be a special guest during their performance, you'll get in front of a crowd, build your name/following, and grab compelling content of you with screaming supporters. Nothing is as swaying to someone on my side of the desk as seeing people react to you, get excited, and interact. This shows us that there is IRL excitement.

4. Submit via our website. I go through these submissions. If DigiTour is coming to your hometown, ask if you can be a local guest on a single date. Especially if you can get people to come out to support you in your hometown, this is a smart move. If you're a new emerging talent without a proven tour history but you can guarantee you'll bring twenty, thirty, or even fifty friends who will buy tickets, this will definitely get my attention!

5. Tweet or DM me or my team. I can't promise we'll always see it, but if you really believe you've got what it takes and you want to lead with your best pitch (remember no second chances for first impressions), reach out, introduce yourself, and go for it!

Selling tickets is a lot harder than you might think. If you have a thousand followers, maybe 10 to 20 percent of them would be up for seeing you live. Out of that remaining two hundred, maybe fifty live close enough to even come to the event, *and* are available to attend, *and* can afford to buy a ticket. If a fan meets all that criteria, they still need to be motivated to actually buy a ticket and show up, rather than stay comfortably at home and watch your content in their sweatpants. Someone can have a million followers, but still only be able to motivate fifty people to buy a ticket.

Tour organizers, like myself, are looking for two types of people to book: someone who sells tickets (meaning someone whose audience is so excited they will easily spring to buy a VIP ticket as soon as we announce), and someone who has a large audience and can spread the word about the tour, the dates, ticket links, and other talent performing. Ideally, the talent we book has both these traits.

Typically we evaluate a talent's ability to sell tickets by booking them as a local guest at one event. Normally we do not pay them for this. If someone is buzzing but we don't have any data on how many tickets they can sell, we'll usually pay their travel fees.

Sometimes we might pay a small fee, a few hundred dollars per show, if we think they'll be able to sell at least a few tickets. Many talent think their brand rates (what brands pay them to post branded content) should be their live appearance rates, but they are never the same. A brand wants one thing and a tour organizer wants another. It's one thing to get eyeballs on social media; it's a totally different thing to be able to get feet in the door.

The larger fees go to the talent we know can sell tickets, and these stars can earn thousands of dollars for every tour date they do. It's not an arbitrary system, and I'm not in the business of handing out money for the fun of it. If I pay someone a lot of money and no one buys tickets, then I won't have that money to spend on an influencer that can actually fill seats. The big bucks go to people who are a proven draw.

The real money made for talent on the road is selling merch. Some of the big talent we work with can clear as much as fifteen thousand dollars per night in merch sales at a sold-out show. Do twenty shows in one month and that's not a bad chunk of change (we'll talk more about merch in the next chapter).

The top talent who have toured before and proven their ability might opt to work with us as a partner. When this happens, DigiTour doesn't guarantee any fee per show, but instead we split profits at the end.

Whatever the arrangement on a fee, or a profit share, plus merch, *plus* sponsorship, touring can be very lucrative for the biggest talent. For the newer talent, it's usually not making you money, but it is making you bigger—you undoubtedly will grow your audience and engagement, and be better positioned to earn big money in the future.

Selfie Made Mode:

- ▶ Team up with other friends who have followings and put on your own live event!

- ▶ Selfie Made transcends social media. Be Selfie Made in every walk of life.

Are You Making $ Yet?

Well? Are you making money yet?

If you haven't gotten your followers and engagement levels up, then odds are, no. But if you have, then perhaps you've received your first inquiry from a brand? Maybe a company wants to send you free stuff? Amazing! Congrats!

I'll go over all the main ways you can make money on social media. It's not about the money for everyone, but if you can make money doing what you love, then why not?!

THE (GROWING) LIVESTREAMING ECONOMY

Livestreaming is often how the early and emerging talent turn their hobby into a bill-paying job. This is your best opportunity to earn one- to three thousand dollars per month to help pay rent, pay for your car, or save up for better gear.

According to an article published in *Adweek* at the tail end of 2016, by the year 2021, livestreaming will be a $70 billion business. There are currently a few livestreaming options, but at this rate, I'm sure there will be a lot more by the time you're reading this. Heck, probably by the time I'm done typing . . . this sentence.

YOUNOW

YouNow has a virtual currency called "bars," which users can purchase and give out as gifts. There are currently six types of gifts: four hundred likes, five hundred likes, applause, tips, fan mail, and marriage proposal. The value of each ranges from a dollar to a hundred dollars. Generally, viewers buy bars at about seven or eight cents each. Any user can receive gifts, but only partnered creators can earn money from them. Top earners on YouNow make $150,000 to $200,000 per year.

LIVE.LY

Live.ly utilizes digital gifts that you can purchase in the form of emojis or coin packs. One hundred coins are currently priced at 99 cents, five hundred coins are priced at $4.99, two thousand coins are priced at $19.99, and so on. The emojis range from five cents to fifty dollars. The higher the cost of the emoji, the more prominently it will be featured in the stream. Broadcasters will tend to shout-out the larger contributions, encouraging fans to continue to gift. Broadcasters are also able to publish a leaderboard to highlight their fans who gifted the most. According to both Mashable and *Variety*, Musical.ly's previous president Alex Hofmann has cited that the top Live.ly broadcasters were making $46,000 in a two-week period using this monetization feature. Not bad!

LIVE.ME

This one is a little confusing, so pay attention. Users convert money into virtual currency called *coins*. Coins can be gifted to broadcasters. Each gift is worth a certain number of diamonds. Let's recap: money turns into coins, which turn into diamonds, and then diamonds can be turned into real money again. Some coins are actually free and can be earned by getting friends to download the app, but many users opt to buy them. Sixty-nine coins = ninety-nine cents. Once a broadcaster receives forty thousand diamonds they are eligible for payout.

TWITCH

The ability to monetize on this video gamer livestreaming platform recently opened up to the masses. Previously it was only available to the top seventeen thousand partners out of their 2.2 million unique users. Twitch offers a few ways to make money:

1. **Subscriptions:** For between $4.99 and $24.99, viewers can opt into exclusive perks, which include chats and "emotes" (small pictures utilized in chat boxes).
2. **Advertising:** Creators can choose frequency of the mid-roll ads and can make $3,000 to $5,000 monthly on this feature.
3. **Emotes:** They call this feature cheering. One hundred bits= $1.40. Users will tip from one hundred to ten thousand bits in a message. In a little less than a year this feature generated $12 million in revenue.

NON-BROADCAST MONETIZATION

One of the first ways influencers made money was through passive ad revenue on YouTube. Then came brand deals, then came merch. YouTube opened the floodgates. Interestingly, nearly every other platform does *not* offer a way to monetize passively or officially at all. None of the platforms are going to help you get a brand deal. This is one reason talent still migrate to YouTube eventually, even if Musical.ly or Instagram was where they popped off.

YOUTUBE

As of 2017 there is a new policy that requires a channel to have ten thousand lifetime views before you're allowed to become a partner and turn on monetization. Once you're a partner and you've hit your ten-thousand-view minimum, you can expect, on average, to receive a four-dollar CPM (cost per mille aka cost per thousand). This equals four dollars per one thousand views. So with an impressive hundred thousand views, you're only making four hundred dollars. You can increase this number by linking up with an MCN (multi-channel network). Often times a MCN is able to leverage their network to get better rates, sometimes six or seven dollars. But really you will need millions of consistent views on weekly content to really rake in the dough. To give you a sense of what this looks like: if you're averaging four million views per video and posting one per week at a preferred six dollar CPM, then you're making just under a hundred thousand dollars per month on ad revenue.

BRAND INTEGRATIONS

The key to making good partnerships with a brand is to manage expectations. You don't want to overpromise what you can do, but you don't want to work for free, either.

When a brand reaches out to you, whether it's a new app seeking downloads, or M&M'S wanting to reach your engaged audience, both are looking at you as a new way to advertise. You have a direct connection to an audience. So that's how they'll look at you: how many people follow you, how many people interact with you (comments, RTs, likes, favs, etc.), and then they'll try to figure out what that may mean for the campaign they want to run. Will your supporters go follow them? Download their app? Buy their product? Go see their movie? Show up at their store?

You know your audience better than any company does, so ask yourself all of the above questions, too. You don't want to be the face of Life Alert when your audience is all in their teens. That wouldn't make sense. What, are you going to throw yourself on the floor and pretend you can't get up? Okay, that might be kind of funny, but that doesn't fit with the brand!

Brands want to be authentic, so if you are in contact with a brand that is interested in promoting to your audience, help that brand *understand* your audience. This is what they want! Find a way to incorporate their message into your posts and content in a way that doesn't feel cringey. Your supporters will support you, they know you need to make money, but don't turn them off with blatant ads. Make it cool.

Another trick is to try and build a campaign with the brand. Doing a single tweet for five hundred or a thousand dollars is cool, but doing a series of posts across platforms and for a period of time for fifteen- or twenty thousand dollars is definitely cooler.

If you're wondering what to charge, there is no written rule as to what paid partnerships cost. Sometimes newer brands will pay a little more, and sometimes trendier brands that can offer perks or that have a large following themselves (free trips, free swag, free promos) will try and negotiate lower fees by including other stuff. No deals are cookie cutter but knowing market value helps provide a starting point. You'll start to get a sense of your market value after you get your first paying brand deal. That will give you a sense of how the advertising market prices/values your following. The real-talk truth of it is they don't *know* your value; they have an algorithm they use, but they're just guessing at it. For a super-savvy creator (or his/her manager) it's about educating a brand about the power of your audience and engagement.

Do some delicate digging when you get an inquiry from a brand. A juice company may want to send you free products to try out on camera. Free products are cool, but if you're effectively serving ads to your audience, you deserve to get paid for that. See if you can turn their offer to send you free products into free products *and* a check. You don't want to scare off opportunities or price yourself too high, but simply asking if there is a budget is a simple, perfectly reasonable response to an inquiry. You can say, "I'd love to try your products, but in order to post on my socials I need some compensation and I'd be happy to work within your budget."

Don't oversell if you want repeat business. Be real, be mature, be about your business. Set expectations and try to overdeliver. If you tell a brand that you can produce X amount of business, and you end up bringing *minus* X, then sure you pulled a quick slick move, but in the words of DJ Khaled, "Congratulations, you played yourself." That could have been a lifelong brand deal, and you turned it into a once and done.

When you're building your social media into a monetizable business, making smart and thoughtful moves will help with longevity.

Let's say you have a small but mighty following, and your business inquiries email is flooded with requests to send you free stuff and do small promos for a few hundred dollars. *Now* would be a good time to find a savvy manager to help you turn the incoming interest into actual income.

You need someone to help be the bad guy and get your rate higher. It can sometimes be hard to do this on your own, especially if you're developing a creative relationship and don't want to make it weird by quibbling over money. An agent or manager can assist you. They work for a percentage of your profits, but they generally will earn you more than you would have gotten on your own, and end up paying for themselves. Rule of thumb: no good agent or manager earns money from you unless you earn money. In other words, be very wary of up-front costs.

Maybe you're ready to take on a branding deal, but haven't been contacted by a brand yet? Make sure you have a business-only contact email in your bio on all your platforms. And if you're feeling extra confident, you may want to bait a brand to notice you. I have seen talent do this successfully.

The downside of a brand deal is they are not something you can always count on in the long term. Because of that, you should always keep streaming. Streaming will provide you with a solid base as you start to diversify your income streams.

MERCH

Merch on the road is certainly a big part of making money, but many social stars also sell in online stores.

If you're just starting, it's a good idea to test out fan-demand. This can help you determine the best course of action. If you create a shirt on CafePress or Merchify that's made to order, you don't have to pay for anything in advance. When your customer orders the shirt, companies like these will print it, on demand. This is a risk-free exercise. You don't have to buy a hundred shirts up-front and hope you can sell them. And you don't have to pay to store these shirts somewhere until they're sold, which can get pricey.

The downside is that you won't make much profit per shirt. This is how it works: these companies will set a baseline price for a shirt, roughly seventeen dollars, plus shipping. You can charge the customer however much you want, but the shirtmaker is taking that seventeen dollars. If you want to turn a profit, you can charge twenty or twenty-five dollars (both reasonable prices for T-shirts in the space), but you're not walking away with much.

Still, these print-on-demand options are a great first step. If you were to graduate from selling one-off concepts and print-to-order, you could link up with a merch company that can provide better rates. Instead of seventeen dollars, you can pay six to eight dollars per shirt, and now if you sell that shirt for twenty-five, you're getting a much better profit.

The thing is, most of the companies that could offer you competitive rates would want to know you could sell more than twenty shirts per month. It's all about volume of sales. They get better rates when shirts are ordered and printed in bulk. Think of it like this: every time they print a logo on a T-shirt, they go to a printer, set up the design, lay it all out, set it all up, and then they get to printing. If they have to go through this whole process for twenty different shirts that are each selling twenty units, it is less cost effective than printing one shirt four hundred times.

Merch is one of the most lucrative categories for talent and once you have some demand and a good partner in place that can give you bulk rates, you can really start to make money. Introduce your fans/supporters to your merch, be proud of it, and go the extra mile. That means sign your merch, use it in contests, and send it to your big influencer friends and see if they'll help spread the word.

Some of the Biggest Influencer Earners in 2016 according to Forbes:

1. PewDiePie: $15M

2. Roman Atwood: $8M

3. Lilly Singh: $7.5M

4. Smosh: $7M

5. Tyler Oakley: $6M

6. Colleen Ballinger aka Miranda Sings: $5M

● ● ●

SUCCESS

Your hard work is paying off and now you're able to start cashing in. If you're posting on YouTube, you may be receiving a Google AdSense check that could be anywhere from a few thousand dollars to twenty-five thousand or even fifty thousand dollars per month (or more). In addition, if you continue to stream, you'll certainly see another ten- to thirty thousand dollars per month from that. Merch can be yielding another ten- to twenty-five thousand dollars per month. And touring can layer in another payday on top. This is about the time your phone will start ringing about book opportunities, brand deals (with bigger budgets), TV/film opportunities, and more! Congratulations! You've made it!

Selfie Made Mode:

- ▷ Livestreaming is the way of the future.
- ▷ There's money to be made in merchandise, and you can start making it now!

The People Behind the Curtain

There are many jobs in the digital media world that don't involve being in front of the camera. If you don't really care so much about being famous, but really just want a cool, good-paying job that deals with social media, you should look into some of these jobs and see if they're a good fit for you.

INFLUENCER/CREATOR/TALENT

This is the star of the show, the person who's making the content and interacting with the audience. This whole book has been about the talent, because nothing would happen without them. It's a lot of pressure, though. "Uneasy lies the head that wears the crown." That's a Shakespeare quote, and I didn't just use it to sound literary. Go for your dreams—that's the only way you'll achieve them. But don't ignore how your dreams change you.

I have a good friend named Hank who was trying to make it as an actor back when I was trying to make it as a singer. He was a talented guy, and had a lot of drive. But he also had a pretty crippling case of anxiety. Every time he went on an audition for a TV role, his whole body would shake and he'd sweat through his shirt.

Being able to deal with high levels of stress comes with the territory when you are a star. Keep this in mind. Can you handle those high levels of anxiety? Are you going to be able to handle having haters? Is it a compromise you're willing to make?

Hank had to realize this on his own. "The dreams I wanted were my dreams from my childhood. I stayed loyal to those dreams, even as I myself changed. When I really looked inward, I realized my needs as a person and the demands of my dreams were too opposed to each other."

Making it big-time in the entertainment industry, no matter what the medium or format, brings a lot of baggage with it. But it also, obviously, comes with a lot of perks. Really take the time to examine what you really want.

Don't forget: if something stops being fun, maybe it's time for you to move on to something else.

VIDEOGRAPHER

When a budding influencer starts out posting content, usually they're using the camera in their computer or propping up their phone on a tripod. But as they get bigger, especially if they're a YouTuber, it becomes necessary to have someone who can film them, and to keep them on a filming schedule.

Videographers are typically paid seventy-five to a hundred and fifty dollars per day. If you're good with a camera and have a good visual eye, this could be a great job for you. The best part is that there's no real experience necessary. You can take courses and yes, that will definitely help, but lots of videographers are self-taught. You should know how to use Final Cut Pro/ Photoshop, but otherwise, you got this.

If you are thinking of going this route, and are hungry to get out there and have your talents seen, you might consider working for free in exchange for a shout-out, and/or getting tagged with credit.

For a videographer, this kind of exposure can be worth the free work.

Your socials will grow, people will recognize your work *and* your affiliation with a large influencer, and hopeful stars will want to book your services (at full price!).

EDITOR

Some videographers double as editors, too. But for the very busy influencer with a demanding video schedule (not to mention several brand-deal vids to deliver, too), someone on staff who can cut together videos as soon as they are shot is extremely helpful.

Editors are typically paid by the hour, or charge a daily rate, or sometimes a flat rate per edited video. Getting close with one influencer and working with them regularly will be most beneficial (for the editor and the influencer).

Just like with videographers, a hopeful editor may agree to take a pay cut or work for gratis for a big client in exchange for social shout-outs, and/or to build a following.

PHOTOGRAPHER

Nearly every influencer needs good photo content for Instagram. Many influencers will partner up with burgeoning photographer talent and in exchange for photo cred, the photog will snap high-resolution shots of the influencer for use on social.

Ever hear of Bryant Eslava? He did this for Cameron Dallas and 2.9 million of his own Insta followers later, he may be the most well-recognized photographer in the influencer space. Bryant took a pay hit in the beginning but is hired left and right now for brand deals, magazine shoots, and more. He invested his time wisely!

MANAGER

Typically, a manager will take 15 percent of what the influencer makes. In exchange, a manager is a key advisor on all business opportunities, and an all-around right hand.

As a manager, you may have a range of responsibilities, from fielding incoming inquiries to assembling the rest of the team, advising on what moves make the most sense, brand vision, etc.

Some managers are like day-to-day pals with their clients, making house calls and traveling with them. Others work out of offices and focus on big-picture decisions. Maybe they'll send an assistant to cover the more daily handholding. It really depends on the needs of the influencer.

Is a manager important? Not initially. Usually a parent or best friend or even a hired assistant can help with the general business requirements. Light maintenance mostly, like responding to business email inquiries, helping to schedule any brand deals, assisting you with your content schedule, organizing your travel, etc. But as an artist gets busier and there are big offers coming in for brand integrations, book deals, PR requests, tour deals, and beyond, they may want someone to help sift through everything, organize, and prioritize.

A manager should be earning their own keep: they make 15 percent of all income, and they should be adding at *least* 10 percent of value to a star's bank account. If they're doing that, then they essentially pay for themselves. That means negotiating higher rates, bringing newer and better opportunities to the table, and making sure contracts say and do what they're supposed to. Through their expertise and connections, good managers contribute to the bottom line.

BUSINESS MANAGER

> Before you get a manager, get a business manager. You don't want to go broke.
> —TREVOR MORAN

You'd be forgiven for thinking a business manager is just a manager who focuses on . . . business. Not exactly. A business manager is a CPA (certified public accountant). This is the person who does an influencer's taxes, but also so much more.

Social stars are usually paid as independent contractors. Basically, if Skittles wants to pay you to promote their product, they're not usually going to make you an employee of Skittles; you're not getting on their benefits plan, you're not coming to the company retreat, you're just performing a service for them and keeping it moving.

This also means Skittles won't take any taxes out of your paycheck. They'll give you the entire amount, and you'll be expected to pay the taxes yourself at the end of the year. In a case like this, Skittles will issue you a 1099 form at the end of the year, which tells the government how much they paid you, and how much the government needs to tax you on.

What does all this mean for the influencer? For every dollar they make, they need to save 30 percent (at least) for their taxes. If they don't know this, when Tax Day comes around, they could get in trouble with the government and even face bankruptcy. Many influencers have learned this the hard way, because they either don't have, or didn't listen to, their business manager. I know one popular YouTuber in particular who didn't save that 30 percent, and couldn't pay his very huge tax bill. He ended up having to move out of his house, and almost filed for bankruptcy.

Properly managing your money, saving, setting up a company (S corp or LLC), and following certain protocols make a business manager *indispensable* to the moneymaking influencer.

Some business managers offer to take 5 percent of earnings, but others charge an affordable hourly rate to manage a star's books, pay their taxes, and help advise on financial matters. Hourly fees can range from a hundred and fifty to three hundred dollars. If you're good with numbers, and looking for a steady living but also the thrill of working with stars, consider going into business management.

LAWYER

Oh boy, lawyers. Maybe this isn't the most fun profession, but a lawyer is a key member of Team Influencer.

They are simply a necessity in the modern world. The nice thing about being a lawyer is that there are so many avenues to go down. No matter where your interests lie, becoming a lawyer can be lucrative.

In the world of social media, lawyers aren't needed for everything, but they are vital when it comes to reviewing brand agreements, tour deals, as well as any other agreements influencers will inevitably need to sign, like a management agreement or a deal from a multi-channel network. Lawyers come in all shapes and sizes and specialties, but in the digital/influencer space, the talent will usually be working with an entertainment lawyer.

Fees can range drastically, usually from two hundred to seven hundred dollars an hour. When influencers ask me to recommend a lawyer, I always suggest opting for someone who seems like a worker bee and is responsible, not the firm with the fanciest lobby.

If you can survive the necessary schooling, and don't mind that everyone will make jokes about how annoying lawyers are, this can be an incredibly rewarding profession. Usually, when big things are happening, there's a lawyer in the room (or on the speakerphone).

PUBLICIST

A publicist will go out to the media (magazines, newspapers, TV shows, radios) and pitch talent for interviews, features, and for red carpet events and hosting. Usually a publicist is paid a monthly fee, which is referred to as a retainer. That retainer can range from twenty-five hundred to ten thousand dollars per month. For an influencer, they shouldn't hire a publicist until they can afford their services.

If you're good at talking to people, if you can put on a positive face and sell anything to anyone, you might make a good publicist. You need to maintain positive relationships with a lot of different people, because you never know who might have a perfect opportunity for your client.

ASSISTANT

As things become more demanding between appearances, traveling to events, brand deals, and a more rigorous posting schedule, it can become daunting for an influencer to handle many of the day-to-day tasks and scheduling on their own. An assistant can be the first member of an influencer's team, even before a manager.

Usually an assistant ranges from twenty to thirty dollars an hour or if they're on salary, thirty- to forty-five thousand dollars per year. For a busy influencer, this is a small price to pay to keep their life on track. To a fresh-out-of-school go-getter who wants to get into the middle of things and learn about how everything works, being an assistant is a great first step.

If you know an influencer who lives in your area, reach out and ask if they have an assistant, or are interested in hiring one. It may not always be a glamorous position, but as with everything, it's all about what you make of it. Plenty of assistants go on to run their own management companies, become lawyers, or even step out in front of the camera and become influencers themselves, utilizing everything they learned while watching from behind the scenes.

AGENT

There are many big and small agencies that represent digital talent. The biggest are CAA, WME, ICM Partners, APA, UTA, and Paradigm Media. Technically, managers can't negotiate work on their client's behalf; they can only legally advise what they think is best. It's the agent's express job to go get their client paying work.

For some time (too long really) big agencies had no idea what to do with social media talent. Was it a passing fad? Could these kids actually make any money? Now they're all hip to the real world, and signing up the hottest new acts before their competition can get there first. Most of the big agencies now have departments devoted to digital talent, which help negotiate content deals with platforms like YouTube or Facebook. There are separate departments that deal with film/TV, books, brand endorsements, and more. A star typically has one agent who wants to represent them, and they'll be known as the RA (responsible agent, aka your point person). If talent signs with an agency across the board (meaning the agency is responsible for agenting deals across digital, film, books, music, everything), multiple people at the company will bring opportunities, but they will flow through an RA. Agents make 10 percent, which is the standard amount. Some agents who focus on specialties make 15 percent.

Some social media star hopefuls are so focused on getting an agent, they lose sight of the fact that an agent can only help you help yourself. They only make 10 percent of what you earn, so if they see talent as needing a lot (or too much) work and growth before there's money to be made, they won't be interested. An influencer doesn't need an agent if they're not ready for paying gigs. I don't mean ready as in emotionally ready; aren't we all ready to get paid? I mean ready as far as demand and size of audience. Agents are only helpful when the phone is ringing!

If you're thinking about being a social media influencer, or have been working at it with little success, branching off into agenting can be a great step. You already understand the mind-set of influencers, you know what the demands are, and you can relate to them. That sounds like the makings of a great agent!

BRANDING AGENT

There are some companies that purely focus on getting brand deals for digital talent, like FameBit, Grapevine, and Digital Brand Architects. If you love the idea of playing matchmaker for a brand and social star, this could be a great job for you!

TOURING PARTNER

This is what yours truly does! DigiTour is in many ways the Live Nation of social media. We are often the first call when talent wants to hit the road. There's a lot that goes into putting together a tour as I listed previously, but basically you are finding and booking talent; picking the right routing (collection of dates/cities); designing the look and feel of the show, and the look and feel of the set; and promoting the tour, i.e. selling tickets. Let's not forget once the tour starts there is the management of all the on-the-road logistics.

Executive Advice with Claudine Cazian (as provided in her own words)

Claudine Cazian (@claudine) is the head of entertainment for Instagram. She is one of the few people who manage Instagram's verified accounts and big partners. I asked her what advice she'd give to Insta users trying to make it big and boy, did she deliver!

How would you compare a traditional platform, like radio, to a social platform like Instagram in terms of reach, impact, and breaking new talent?

Traditional platforms, like radio, and social media platforms, like Instagram, are fairly similar when it comes to creating a loyal fan base, a personal narrative, and most important, a community. While the two may seem *very different*, both rely on three main principles: **authenticity, consistency,** and **developing a voice.**

♥ **Authenticity** is your ability to be real with your audience. Specifically, it's *what* you share, *how* you share it, and, most important, the *why* behind it. For example: Why do you choose to show your highlights and also the moments in between on Instagram? It's because you want your followers to know that they're just like you and going through similar life experiences and challenges. The easiest way to do that? Be honest and open.

♥ **Consistency** is your ability to share *all* moments with your fans *in real time*. It means making the commitment to show the various areas of your life—the ones you're proud of *and* the ones that need work—in a thoughtful and consistent way. The easiest way to do that? Give people a glimpse into your daily life_and don't be overly curated!

♥ Lastly, **developing a voice** is key. This is your time to reflect and ask yourself what you *really* care about and commit to sharing it with the world in an honest and authentic way. The easiest way to do this? Document your life; don't produce it. Commit to sharing the inner voice inside your head without overthinking it and, of course, trust your gut.

Any insider tips for increasing your following?

A great way to engage your followers and grow your fan base is to really lean in to all of the awesome surfaces Instagram has to offer:

♥ Go Live

♥ Use Stories daily

♥ Upload several pieces of Feed and Video content

♥ Be consistent

♥ Be part of the global conversation

♥ Collaborate with other Instagrammers you like or have an interest in knowing

♥ And, most important, lend your voice in a positive and productive manner

Is photo or video better for engagement?

A healthy mix of content is key, but there has been a substantial increase in video, so it's important to make sure video is a key component of your strategy. First-person point of view content is ideal. You want your fans to know that you're the one shooting this content and that it's personal to you. Stay away from anything that's overly produced or too slick. Just be real, and a smartphone is all you need.

Is there an ideal video length?

My rule of thumb: ensure that your content is "tight and bright." Bottom line: only include content that is necessary to moving your story or narrative forward. Cut anything that is considered excess.

What's the ideal number of posts per day?

Post what you love in a consistent manner and don't overthink it. The goal: document your life and have fun!

What are the best kinds of photos to post?

The best content, hands down, is personal content—*photos, videos,* and *Lives of you and your actual life.* This is the good stuff that people really want to see! I always recommend a good 80/20: 80 percent personal content and 20 percent promotional content for the projects you're working on.

What are your favorite Instagram trends?

Video on Instagram has really exploded; it's one of the biggest trends we've seen in the last year. Motion is the new filter. Think about it: isn't it nearly impossible to scroll past a Boomerang on your feed? It's because video provides a deeper and more engaging way to tell your story (not to mention the fact that it's just fun). There's a really fun rewind functionality to Instagram Stories. Live is another area we're really excited about. With Lives you can connect in the moment, whether that's watching Ansel Elgort on his global movie tour, or sharing a moment with Justin Bieber singing in his car.

Tell me the truth about hashtags: do they help? Can too many hurt?

Hashtags are a great way to have your content discovered—*and now, you can even follow hashtags*—but there's no need to overuse them or get too broad. For example: if you're attending New York Fashion Week, using #fashion is too general, but using #NYFW is way more specific and targeted. I also recommend creating your own hashtag for content that you plan to produce on a weekly/consistent basis.

Boomerang advice: what makes a great one?

The trick to Boomerang: make one movement and let the camera do the rest!

Insta Story is taking over. What's your best advice to use it for growth?

I love Instagram Stories because it's a great way to share the everyday moments of your life in a really low-key way. (Bonus: it only lives for twenty-four hours, but you can choose to archive it in your _Stories highlights_ if you want to!) To date, we have more than three hundred million active Stories users per day, so it's important to post to your Stories tray daily! Tip: choose three to five things that you do every week and share those areas of your life consistently. For example: if you like to have coffee with friends, show it. If you like a particular workout class, show it. If you enjoy time exploring your city, show it and create a custom hashtag for that content! Consistency is key and don't be afraid of showing the everyday moments in your life—that's what people ultimately want.

For someone interested in working at a social platform, what advice can you give?

Working at a tech company is fast paced, exciting, and definitely a 24/7 job. In previous and more traditional roles, I've always laid out my full business plan for the year, but in this job, I have to make sixty to ninety plans and be ready to pivot at any moment. Why? Because the technology is always changing and I need to be ready to adapt at a moment's notice. It's one of the things I love most about working in tech.

In your role, do you work directly with talent? What do you focus on in your role?

As the head of entertainment for Instagram, I work closely with the full entertainment community: actors/actresses, TV shows, and movies. It's a dream job! I work closely with each to give them best practices on the platform and, most important, help them engage with their fans in a two-way manner that's meaningful for all. The core of Instagram is based on *community* and I work to help them build and engage with that community.

What does a day in your life look like?

4:50 A.M.: Alarm goes off, with time for one *snooze* button!

5:00 A.M.: Quick scan of my Instagram Stories tray, then a scroll through Feed. (I'm often still blurry eyed!)

5:15 A.M.: Leave my house.

5:30 A.M.: Pilates class. (It's important for me to get a workout first thing in the morning!)

6:30 A.M.: Post an IG story on my handle @claudine.

6:40 A.M.: Get ready for work.

7:15 A.M.: Have breakfast with my daughter.

8:00 A.M.: Depart for school drop-off.

8:30 A.M.: At the office, a quick scan of email, then I address urgent matters that surfaced overnight.

9:00 A.M.: Instagram Partnerships team meeting. (My favorite meeting of the week, as it's a chance for me to connect with my global counterparts. They are all incredibly smart, kind, and driven.)

10:00 A.M.: Meet with my entertainment team for one hour while we plan out our top three of the week. We meet on Mondays to collectively determine the three things we need to accomplish that week. This is a great tip and keeps us focused on our goals.

11:00 A.M.: One-on-one talent meeting at the office.

12:30 P.M.: Quick lunch at the office café. (I try not to work while eating lunch, but often do!)

1:00 P.M.: Quick check of texts, pings, and, of course, my Instagram. (I average several hundred pieces of incoming per day.)

2:00 P.M.: Another talent or partner meeting.

4:00 P.M.: Catch up on the hundreds of emails that have amassed during my meetings.

6:00 P.M.: Depart to have dinner at home with my family.

8:00 P.M.: Put my daughter to sleep.

8:30 P.M.: Catch up on emails, attend an industry event, or catch up with my husband!

10:00 P.M.: In bed, a quick final scan of my Instagram (of course!) and lights out.

BEGINNERS

I know, you just read about how you're going to need a lawyer, and now you're kind of freaking out. Seems like a lot of steps between now and when you'll need financial counsel ponied up next to you. But that's okay. Trust me, when you need to have a lawyer, you'll know. For now, focus on the steps we've talked about throughout this book, put together a plan, and as things get more complicated, you'll at least have a working understanding of what to expect.

There's a lot of information I've packed into this book, and as you go through your social media career, different parts will be of use to you. Don't let the distance to your goals be a deterrent. Remember, all it takes is a tipping point and you're there!

PROS

As you grow, get bigger, attract more attention, and enter into deals and partnerships, you're bound to meet a few bad apples. The old expression is true: "more money, more problems." But even more so: more responsibility, more problems.

The people you deal with and do deals with can turn on you, and learning who to trust is paramount. Remember, not every smile is real, and what's best for you is not necessarily what is best for someone else. The day someone puts a contract in front of you will be a day of lots of smiles and hugs . . . but what happens if the project doesn't do well? Things don't always work out and managing through it with good people makes all the difference.

This is why having a good manager and/or agent is so important. This is why having a lawyer to make sure every contract you sign is by the book is worth five hundred dollars an hour. When you're gathering your team, make sure you take your time. I've had some incredible partners and team members and I've also had some of the worst. You need to analyze partnerships and not jump in too quickly. When you're thinking of working with someone ask yourself the following:

1. Do you share a similar vision for the project?

2. Do you trust them? Will they tell you when you have spinach in your teeth?

3. Do they know how to communicate? If they tend to go MIA, you're probably better off without them.

4. Do they have a good reputation? Can they provide references? Do you know anyone who's worked with them before? Never underestimate the power of a reference. If someone gives you one to call, call that reference!

When I hire new staff at DigiTour I always ask two questions:

"What would your ideal job be if you could have any job today?"

This answer can be really telling. What is their long-term goal? If I'm a social media star and my manager is looking to start a social media brand, maybe they're not the right fit for me. They may be more focused on their own social brand than mine, and could be conflicted sending me new opportunities if they secretly want them for themselves.

The next question I ask is, "What do you want from this job?" Since you are reading this book, I'll even give you the best answer:

"I want to grow as much as I can within this job and I want to learn."

If they're just bored and looking for something to do, that's a big no from me. Sorry, dude. I want people around me who are motivated because they will make the most out of the opportunity. If you don't have a drive in you, then that's like waving a big red flag in my face that says I WILL WASTE YOUR TIME. DigiTour is a fast-paced company; you have to keep up the pace or someone else will (my Miranda Priestly moment).

Selfie Made Mode:

- ▷ Be aware of the different types of jobs in the social media world, and if any of them are right for you, go for it!

- ▷ When the time comes to hire staff, don't rush into it. These are major decisions.

Your
Second
Act

You've made it. You're on top, you're a star, you're everything.

Here's the rub: when you're on top, there's only one way to go. Down, down, down. That's right, the glitter and the glamour can lead you right down the gutter toward downtown. Not a fancy gentrified downtown, either. I mean a grimy, mean streets kind of downtown.

While it may seem like the excitement and attention of your fandom will never go away, the reality is that a lot of new talent every year end up burning out.

Burning out means they've lost their momentum. Maybe the pressure of the moment got to them and they had to back off. Or maybe they were unable to keep up the pace, or keep it fresh, or any one of a million other things that they didn't do but somehow, someway, apparently should have known how to do.

When this happens, an influencer gets labeled with that oh-so-awful word that no one wants to think is possible: *irrelevant*.

You know how you go to McDonald's, and their fries are so good, but you don't eat them all, so you put them in the fridge and heat them up later, but they are no longer desirable at all?

That's what it's like. You become yesterday's news. The once-stacked inbox of inquiries for brand deals and appearances dries up. Your collabs are scarce and your engagement level is down the tubes.

Have I scared you? Good! If you're lucky enough to get to influencer status and make a career in social media, you better be smart enough to know how to plan ahead and prepare for what I like to call *Your Second Act*. Even if you make it past year one and year two and continue to grow your popularity, it's inevitable at some point that your audience is going to go to college, age out, and find other interests.

If you're the one in a million who doesn't have this happen, well high-five this page and pretend it's me! Congrats! But for most of you out there, let's plan for the future.

The key is this: at the peak of your popularity, begin to plant seeds. Structure deals that will benefit you in the long run, not the one-thousand-dollars-for-a-tweet deals, but the *equity in an app* deal, or the merchandise-in-Target deal, or the branching out and creating another O&O (owned and operated business) that you lend your name/influence to that has the opportunity to grow and pay out over time deal.

To do any of this, you need the right people behind you, but remember: you're the one who has to deliver the goods.

MY COVER STORY MOMENT

I was asked to be on the inaugural cover of popular teen mag *J-14*'s new offshoot, *Teen Boss*. Me, a cover model. It brought up a lot of feels. However, I knew enough to know that my own personal feelings were involved, which makes things messy, so I needed to bring someone else into the conversation. I sat down with Chris and told him about the offer.

"What's the problem? It sounds great," Chris said.

"Come on, this doesn't even make sense. I myself am no longer a teen; what would I be doing on the cover of a teen magazine?"

"Yeah, but you always say you're fourteen at heart, don't you?"

"Okay, so I guess I'll rip out my heart and they can photograph that."

Chris stopped talking—the conversation clearly wasn't heading anywhere productive. But it did get me thinking.

That night I thought about what I was so worked up about. There was a time when I wanted nothing more than to be on a magazine

Teen Boss *photo shoot*

cover. Here it was, being offered, and it felt like the dream of another girl, not me. My dreams had shifted, it didn't seem right to have the outcome work out the same.

I looked over at Chris, who was wrapped up in *Shark Tank*, like we always are.

"DigiTour means a lot to teens," I said.

"Yes, it does," Chris replied.

"Most of our talent are teens."

"That's true."

"I guess I have some advice that could prove helpful to some people."

Chris smiled. "I think you're right."

"Okay, I'll do it."

The next day I reached out to the editors at *Teen Boss* and told them I'd be happy to be on the cover of their magazine, but I had one catch: I was bringing my talent with me. I then called some of our talent, including some from the tour

Teen Boss *photo shoot*

Teen Boss *cover*

we were on for DigiTour Winter 2017, to join me in the magazine limelight: Tyler Brown, Nathan Triska, and Simon Britton. And Kristen Hancher, who wasn't on tour at the time but was a friend to the company.

They were all superexcited, none of them had ever been on a magazine cover before, either. As I called each of them, I thought about how far I had come. My conversations with the talent now were so different than when Chris and I started DigiTour. Now I was Mom to them. That's why I needed them there with me: at the end of the day, it's the talent that drives my business, and it's my job to make them shine.

The photo shoot for the cover was set to take place in New York City, on the same day as our sold-out show at the Gramercy Theatre. I reached out to some contacts I have at Forever 21 and they let me come in to pull looks. That means they let me walk into their three-story store in Times Square with my assistant in tow, and we picked out clothes for myself and all the talent for the photo shoot. I began slowly, looking discerningly at each T-shirt, different styles of ripped jeans, and trendy jackets, but by the end I looked more like the Tasmanian Devil: a swirling ball of speed, adrenaline, and on-trend outfits piled higher than my eye line.

I selected about eight bags of stuff, from chokers, to heels, to jeans and jackets, and we loaded them in the car. For Forever 21, giving us these clothes was a good price to pay in exchange for the publicity: a magazine has their clothes on the cover. It's a win-win, a perfect example of a successful collab.

We picked up clothes from a few other stops, too: Ralph Lauren, Marissa Webb, and Barneys New York. In my hotel I set up a rack in the oversized bathroom and started to mix and match all the outfits for myself and all the talent.

The next day we sat in hair and makeup, played dress-up, and headed to the Gramercy Theatre. The photographer asked me to stand in the middle, surrounded by the social stars. I smiled as wide as my face would let me, and silently hoped I didn't look ridiculous.

After the shoot was done, I changed back into my actual show outfit: black sneakers, black T-shirt, and black jeans with a walkie-talkie attached to them. It felt comforting to be back in my own clothes. Meridith Rojas, International Cover Model, was a surreal experience. Running around putting out figurative (and sometimes literal) fires so that thousands of teens can have the best night of their life? That's what I do, and I *love* what I do. But now I had blended my aspirations for on-cam success with my materialized dreams of being the boss. That's exactly what Gen Z success is all about: being the creator/influencer/talent *and* the boss.

As a promotion for the magazine, *Teen Boss* had me host a chat with my co-models, where we could talk about our respective online businesses. We also did magazine signings with Barnes & Noble, including a red carpet, which I walked down in a dress. I stood in a meet & greet line with the talent, my first time being in one, and it was exhilarating. It also had my phone going nuts with notifications on my socials. So many of the girls who went through the line having no idea who I was, came out of there knowing all about Meridith Rojas and DigiTour. And they reposted the photos they took with me, sharing gratitude and excitement for DigiTour. My own social numbers went up drastically, proving firsthand the impact a meet & greet has on social following. That was just one night: multiply that times twenty tour dates and the result is real and something quantifiable.

None of this will come easily, but that's something everyone will tell you.

Still, I know, it's one thing to be told it's hard, and it's another thing to find out for yourself, so you just go find out for yourself.

The people who say these things though? They don't really know as much about the internet as Gen Z does. If you're Gen Z, you're a native social user, you speak the language, you understand the customs. A couple of the generations before you are right there with you, the ones that grew up on analog but switched to digital in their younger years. But for the most part, the people who are running the big businesses see the digital landscape as foreign territory. The internet has made all the old rules obsolete, and it's up to you to create new ones.

What nobody will tell you is that you might one day see yourself doing something you never imagined. DigiTour is not what I ever imagined I would be doing, but that doesn't mean it's not what I was meant to do: *I just hadn't imagined it yet*. I've never doubted that I made the right decision, but then, I've never doubted that my business would be successful. And in time I may be doing something completely different. I've learned to always keep my options open.

Keep an open mind. Go where the wind takes you. Relax, take a breath. Think before you text. Never internet angry. Take it easy on yourself. Forgive people for being human. Put in the work. Overnight viral success is a long shot that can never be counted on. Put in the work. Put in the work. Put in the work.

GOOD-BYE FOR NOW!

Wow, that was a whirlwind. We got through a lot of material here, so if you're feeling overwhelmed, don't be! Go back and reread the sections that pertain to where you are right now. Use the pages in the back of this book to put your plan together, and act on it!

I'm not one for soppy, long-winded good-byes, so I'm just going to leave it right here.

Go out and be Selfie Made! Use #SelfieMade to interact with me and keep me up to date with your progress. Good luck, and I can't wait to see you on the road, headlining with DigiTour!

These next pages are for you to explore. Create a sample schedule, describe what you would like your brand to be . . . take the first step . . . and plan!

Selfie Made Planning Pages

✦ ✦ ✦

Brainstorm some sample schedules and see what works for you!

_____
_____
_____
_____
_____
_____
_____
_____
_____
_____
_____
_____
_____
_____
_____
_____
_____

Track your followers on each platform.

_____

_____

_____

_____

_____

_____

_____

_____

_____

Use this space to jot down content ideas.

_____

_____

_____

_____

_____

_____

_____

_____

What makes you, you? That is your brand. Write it all down here.

_____

_____

_____

_____

_____

_____

_____

_____

Name your fandom!

If you need help, take the first half of your name and add one of the following suffixes:

-inators

-izers

-iners

-ies

-army

_____

_____

_____

_____

_____

For more #Selfie Made planning tips, tricks, and exclusive content, visit selfiemadeceo.com.